London

by Paul Murphy

Paul Murphy's first London guide won the
London Tourist Board award for the best
London guidebook of the year. Since then he
has written over 40 guidebooks to holiday
destinations all over the world and has
contributed to many more books and
publications. London, however, is still
his favourite place.

Above: *A Chelsea pensioner*

AA Publishing

On guard in Whitehall

Written by Paul Murphy

First published 1999
Reprinted 2001. Information verified and
updated. Reprinted May 2002; April 2003.
Reprinted 2004. Information updated and
verified. Reprinted May, Jul and Dec 2004
**Reprinted 2006. Information verified and
updated.**
Reprinted Feb, June and July 2007

© Automobile Association Developments
Limited 2006

Published by AA Publishing, a trading name of Automobile
Association Developments Limited, whose registered office
is Fanum House, Basing View, Basingstoke, Hampshire,
RG21 4EA.
Registered number 1878835.

Enabled by | Ordnance Survey   This product includes mapping data
licensed from Ordnance Survey®
with the permission of the Controller of Her Majesty's
Stationery Office. © Crown copyright 2007. All rights
reserved. Licence number 100021153.

A CIP catalogue record for this book is available from the
British Library.

Find out more about
AA Publishing and the
wide range of travel
publications and services
the AA provides by
visiting our website at
www.theAA.com/travel

A03510

Colour separation: Keenes, Andover
Printed and bound in Italy by Printer Trento S.r.l.

Contents

About this Book 4

Viewing London 5–14

Paul Murphy's London 6
London's Features 7
Essence of London 8–9
The Shaping of London 10–11
Peace and Quiet 12–13
London's Famous 14

Top Ten 15–26

British Museum 16–17
Covent Garden Piazza 18
Houses of Parliament 19
National Gallery 20
Natural History Museum 21
St. Paul's Cathedral 22
Science Museum 23
Tower of London 24
Victoria and Albert Museum 25
Westminster Abbey 26

What to See 27–90

Central London 30–77
In the Know 52–53
Food and Drink 60–61
Outer London and Beyond 78–90

Where To... 91–116

Eat and Drink 92–99
Stay 100–103
Shop 104–109
Take the Children 110–111
Be Entertained 112–116

Practical Matters 117–124
Index 125–126
Acknowledgements 126

About this Book

KEY TO SYMBOLS

🚻 map reference to the maps in the What to See section

✉ address

☎ telephone number

🕐 opening times. Note: May–Oct refers to 1 May to 31 October

🍴 restaurant or café on premises or near by

Ⓔ nearest underground train station

🚌 nearest bus/tram route

🚉 nearest overground train station

⛴ nearest ferry stop

ℹ tourist information

♿ facilities for visitors with disabilities

✋ admission charge

❓ other practical information

➤ indicates the page where you will find a fuller description

This book is divided into five sections to cover the most important aspects of your visit to London.

Viewing London pages 5–14
An introduction to London by the author
London's Features
Essence of London
The Shaping of London
Peace and Quiet
London's Famous

Top Ten pages 15–26
The author's choice of the Top Ten places to see in London, listed in alphabetical order, each with practical information.

What to See pages 27–90
Two sections: Central London and Outer London and Beyond, each with its own brief introduction and an alphabetical listing of the main attractions
Practical information
Snippets of 'Did you know…' information
6 suggested walks
2 features

Where To... pages 91–116
Detailed listings of the best places to eat, stay, shop, take the children and be entertained.

Practical Matters pages 117–124
A highly visual section containing essential travel information.

Maps
All map references are to the individual maps found in the What to See section of this guide.
For example, Buckingham Palace has the reference 🚻 28C2, indicating the page on which the map is located and the grid square in which the royal residence is to be found. A list of the maps that have been used in this travel guide can be found in the index.

Prices
Where appropriate, an indication of the cost of an establishment is given by **£** signs:
£££ denotes higher prices, **££** denotes average prices, while **£** denotes lower charges.

Star Ratings
Most of the places described in this book have been given a separate rating:
✪✪✪ Do not miss
✪✪ Highly recommended
✪ Worth seeing

Viewing
London

Paul Murphy's London   6

London's Features   7

Essence of London   8

The Shaping of
   London   10

Peace and
   Quiet   12

London's
   Famous 14

Above: *Trafalgar Square*
Right: *City policeman*

5

Paul Murphy's London

London may be the oldest of the modern world's great cities, with an exceptionally high proportion of ancient buildings, but it is also changing and evolving into a fresher, more vibrant destination for visitors. Some 40 years on from London's Swinging Sixties, the national and international press are telling us that once again this is the place to be.

Leading the world in fashion, music and the arts, London is now also rated as the restaurant capital of the world. Hyperbole or reality? Just look around. Ten years ago, when I wrote my first guide to London, the vast majority of visitor attractions were 'look but don't touch', you couldn't get a decent meal without paying the earth, a cappuccino was still an exotic novelty, beer or wine was off limits for much of the day, and the only way to get into Buckingham Palace was to scale its walls.

Today, London is more European, more worldly, more open in its outlook. The great London institutions of the British Museum, the Tower of London, the museums of South Kensington, and the Royal Opera House have all undergone major improvements. New landmarks such as the BA London Eye grace the skyline and London's developing South Bank and Docklands are also springing to life. Meanwhile, visitors returning to the capital can rest assured that the unsung heroes of London life—the quiet leafy squares, the parks and its myriad tiny unspoilt churches, pubs and shops—soldier timelessly on.

Seeing London

If you want to see London, as opposed to just 'doing' its sights, then put on your walking shoes. The bus and the tube have their uses but you can cover a surprising amount of the central area quite comfortably on foot. It is rarely worth taking the tube for fewer than three stops. The best bits of buildings are often at first-floor level, so keep glancing upwards.

Above: *Narrowboats on the Regent's Canal, built in 1820 to link London's docks to the city of Birmingham*

Right: *Steel and glass at Canary Wharf, the heart of London's new 'City on the Water'*

London's Features

Geography
• London is the largest city in Europe, a ragged oval stretching over 50km (31 miles) across. However, most of 'Visitors' London' is condensed into Inner London, the area bounded by the underground's Circle Line (➤ 72).
• The best way to see the capital is by a combination of underground (tube) and walking.

Locals and Visitors
• London's population reached a peak of around 8.6 million in 1939 then declined slowly to below 7 million in 1983. Only recently has it started to grow again.
• Formerly the world's most populous conurbation, London now ranks number 20 in the world. However, it is still the biggest city in Europe.
• In 1991 London registered 16 million visitors (ie those staying at least one night); by 2004 this figure had increased to 27 million.
• London is a cosmopolitan city, with almost 30 per cent of its population comprising minority ethnic groups.

Problems
• Westminster Council (which deals with the most-visited part of the capital) removes over 90 tons of rubbish per day from its streets.
• London holds the richest and poorest segments of the British population—seven out of ten of the country's most deprived local authorities are in the capital.

Traffic Congestion
The average vehicle speed in London today is 16kph (10mph), not much faster than it was in 1900! Some 5 million people per day choose to ride on the bus and tube network. Congestion charges in the 'inner ring' of the city are now in force on weekdays (7am–6.30pm) to ease the traffic problems.

Government
• Londoners have only recently restored city-wide government. Political wrangling in the 1980s had led to the previous Greater London Council being abolished by central government.
• Most local decisions are devolved to 32 borough councils.
• Croydon is the largest borough with over 330,000 residents. The City of London, covering the square mile in the financial centre, is the smallest with barely 4,000.

Above: *The Houses of Parliament, once described by Tsar Nicholas I as 'a dream in stone'*

Essence of London

London is such a varied and cosmopolitan city that there is a bewildering choice of things to do and see. Perhaps inevitably, visitors feel compelled to tick off its major sights at breakneck speed, but this is no way to get the flavour of the city. The key is not to rush, not to feel you have to see it all (you never will) and not to overlook the simple indigenous pleasures of London. Just for a day or two, forget the museums, the historical attractions, and especially the crowded West End stores. Instead, rummage through a street market stall, stroll in the parks, enjoy a pint in a theme-free pub—in short, be a local.

Below: *Sandwiches in the park and market stall browsing are the locals' ways of spending their lunch hour*

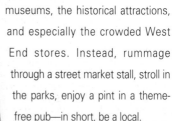

THE 10 ESSENTIALS

If you have only a short time to visit London, or would like to get a real flavour of the city, here are the essentials:

- **Ride on the top deck of a London bus**—still a great way to see the capital. The Big Bus Company operates excellent tours, or take the regular service (No. 11) from Chelsea to Bank.
- **Cruise on the Thames**— London's most under-utilized highway is the perfect route to Greenwich, and the journey is accompanied by a lively commentary.
- **Relax in the park** when the traffic noise grates and your feet ache; escape to Hyde Park, Kensington Gardens, St. James's Park or Regent's Park.
- **Join a walking tour** and let a professional guide take you by the hand and lead you through the streets of London. It is the best and most enjoyable way to learn about the capital—and cheap too. Pick up a flyer from a tourist information office or see *Time Out* for details.

- **Take afternoon tea**—the quintessential British afternoon pastime (➤ 93).
- **Attend a church concert**. Even the least God-fearing of folk will find this an uplifting experience (➤ 113).
- **Enjoy the view from Waterloo Bridge** to see St. Paul's and the London skyline at their very best.
- **Visit a traditional London pub**, although it's hard to tell the phoneys from the real thing these days (➤ 53, 97 for some suggestions).
- **Visit a street market**— two of the best are Brick Lane and Portobello Road, held on Sunday (➤ 108–109 for more suggestions). All London life is there!
- **Visit the Inns of Court**— not a 'sight' as such, but an astonishing oasis in the heart of the city and a glimpse of 'olde London' that few locals (let alone visitors) ever see (➤ 47–48).

Transports of delight—the only thing better than the top deck of a London bus is the top deck of a London boat

The Shaping of London

AD43
The Roman emperor Claudius invades Britain and establishes the deep-water port of Londinium.

c60–200
The Romans build an imperial city and in around AD200 erect a wall around Londinium. The population reaches 45–50,000.

AD410
Romans finally withdraw, leaving Britons to defend themselves. Germanic tribes begin to colonise most of England.

AD851–980
Vikings invade, occupy and destroy much of London. In AD886 King Alfred recaptures and rebuilds the city, establishing it as an international trading centre, but in 980 the Vikings retake it.

1066
The Norman Conquest. William I defeats King Harold at the Battle of Hastings and is crowned King of England at Westminster Abbey.

1176–1209
London Bridge is the first stone bridge to be built in the capital.

1265
The first meeting of 'the Commons' marks the beginnings of the Parliamentary system.

1348
The Black Death, a cocktail of various plagues spread by infected fleas on rats, kills some 75 million people across Eurasia and wipes out around 25–30,000 Londoners (roughly half the population).

1485–1603
Under Tudor rule London becomes Europe's fastest-growing city, with huge growth in trade and commerce. Around 1590 London's original 'Theatreland' is built on the South Bank in Southwark; the West End also takes shape.

1642–49
The English Civil War ends with the execution of Charles I at Whitehall in 1649. Cromwell's forces assume power until the restoration of the monarchy in 1660.

1665
The Great Plague, London's second catastrophic bubonic plague, ravages London and claims the lives of over 100,000 people.

1666
The Great Fire of London burns down 80 per cent of the city's buildings.

St. Paul's is destroyed in the Great Fire of London

10

The Great Exhibition in the Crystal Palace

1750
Westminster Bridge becomes the second bridge across the Thames in London.

1801
The first London census records a population of over 1 million, making it the world's most populous conurbation.

1811–17
As the population continues to explode 14 more bridges are built across the Thames.

1829
Sir Robert Peel establishes the capital's first police force—the Metropolitan Police, (known initially as 'Peelers'). The first London bus service commences.

1834
The Palace of Westminster (Houses of Parliament) burns down.

1849–58
Insanitary living conditions lead to a cholera epidemic which kills 14,000, and river pollution causes 'The Great Stink', which prompts the building of London's first sewerage system. The Great Exhibition opens, in 1851, in Hyde Park.

1863
The world's first urban underground railway runs from Farringdon Street to Edgware Road.

1939–45
During the Blitz of 1940–41 London is bombed for 57 consecutive nights causing 9,500 deaths and much destruction.

1960s
The Beatles are at the forefront of 'Swinging London' and world fashion focuses on Carnaby Street and the King's Road.

1981
Work begins to revive London's Docklands.

1994
Eurostar trains connect London and Paris via the Channel Tunnel.

2002
Queen Elizabeth II celebrates her Golden Jubilee.

2003
Congestion charging introduced to central London's roads.

2005
London successful in bid to stage the 2012 Olympics.

Peace & Quiet

Like all big cities, London can become extremely wearing after just a short time so it's good to know that it has proportionately more green spaces than any other metropolis, plus a fair number of unusual bolt holes.

Hampstead Heath is Londoners' favourite spot for countryside walks without leaving town

Parks and Gardens

Battersea Park What could be more restful than a stroll in a park with a Peace Pagoda of its very own? There's also a children's zoo and a boating pond. Completely off the tourist path yet visible from Chelsea Embankment, the park (and pagoda) is just a few minutes' walk across Albert Bridge (➤ 36).

Chelsea Physic Garden This charming small botanical garden was founded by the Society of Apothecaries; its name means 'of things natural' (➤ 36).

Greenwich Park Lovely gardens, a boating lake and a wonderful view from the top of the hill (➤ 84).

Hampstead Heath/Richmond Park You'll always be able to find space of your own on London's largest heath (➤ 43) or in its largest and wildest park (➤ 87).

Wimbledon Common over 400ha (1,000 acres) of open space in south London: parkland, woodland and heath.

Hampton Court The beautiful grounds and gardens start to fill up at weekends and holidays, but otherwise are delightfully tranquil (► 85).

Hyde Park Too central and too well-known to offer real peace and quiet, but wander into the centre of the park on a weekday in school term time and you might just find a measure of tranquillity. You can hire rowing boats on the Serpentine (► 45).

Kew Gardens The perfect place for those with green fingers—though it does get busy on Sundays (► 86).

The Regent's Canal Take a traditional narrowboat to explore London's backwaters. The most popular excursion (summer only) is from Little Venice to Camden Lock, with London Zoo en route. London Waterbus Company ☎ (020) 7482 2660 or Jason's Trip ☎ (020) 7286 3428.

The statue of Peter Pan in Kensington Gardens was erected overnight as a surprise for the local children

Urban Escapes

Even in the heart of London you'll find unexpected places of calm. Many churches, particularly in the City, have restful small gardens. At lunchtimes free concerts are often given. St. Paul's Churchyard, in Covent Garden (► 18), is a notable oasis and Postman's Park, in Aldersgate (near the Museum of London) is a particularly touching spot with a wall of plaques dedicated to members of the public who died in heroic acts of self-sacrifice.

Under-visited galleries and museums include Apsley House (► 32), Dickens House (► 39), Leighton House (► 50), the National Army Museum (► 59) and the Wallace Collection (► 76).

Thames Path

Officially launched in 1996, the Thames Path is a footpath which allows walkers to follow the Thames all the way from its source (in Gloucestershire) to the Thames Barrier. Follow the South Bank while in central London, though both sides of the river are accessible. National Trail Officer ☎ (01865) 810224, website: www.nationaltrails.gov.uk

Little bits of greenery are found in unexpected places, here next to St. Paul's Cathedral

London's Famous

Charles Dickens

Born on the south coast in Portsmouth in 1812, Charles Dickens came to London in 1823. His early career as a lawyer and a reporter, combined with the financial hardships suffered by his father (who spent a short time in a debtors' prison), shaped his conceptions of the harsh realities and social injustices of London. His first real writing success, under the pen-name Boz, was *The Pickwick Papers*, published in serial form during 1836–37. He went on to write a further 13 major novels, including *A Christmas Carol, Oliver Twist* and *David Copperfield*, and died in 1870 leaving the last one incomplete. A superb orator who took his stories on tour, Dickens was the finest writer of his time and arguably the greatest- ever English novelist. The vitality with which he invested his characters and his ability to tell a story which captured the spirit of the age made him indeed 'The Inimitable'—his own immodest sobriquet! (➤ 39).

Sir Christopher Wren

A brilliant polymath, Christopher Wren (1632–1723) began his career as an astronomer and mathematician before turning to architecture. In 1669 he was appointed Surveyor of Rebuilding after the Great Fire of London. However, contrary to popular legend, his grand plans for a cohesive new London foundered on the complex network and politics of land ownership. Instead he turned his immense talents and energy to St Paul's Cathedral (➤ 22) and to City churches.

Right: Sir Christopher Wren is buried in St. Paul's Cathedral, his most famous work
Below: Her Majesty Queen Elizabeth II

Queen Elizabeth II

London's most famous resident, from April to mid-August at least, is Elizabeth Mountbatten-Windsor, better known as Her Majesty Queen Elizabeth II (born 1926). The rest of the year she recides at Windsor Castle and her other palaces. Despite the family problems of the 1990s—fire at Windsor Castle, the breakdown of three of her children's marriages, the death of Princess Diana, and a widespread appraisal of the modern role of the royals—the Queen remains seemingly inviolable. Sadly, 2002 saw the deaths of her sister and her mother, but also her Golden Jubilee, which bought great celebrations throughout the country.

Top Ten

British Museum	16
Covent Garden Piazza	18
Houses of Parliament	19
National Gallery	20
Natural History Museum	21
St. Paul's Cathedral	22
Science Museum	23
Tower of London	24
Victoria and Albert Museum	25
Westminster Abbey	26

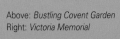

Above: *Bustling Covent Garden*
Right: *Victoria Memorial*

1
British Museum

 29D4

 Great Russell Street, Bloomsbury

(020) 7323 8000; www.british-museum.ac.uk

Main museum Sat–Wed 10–5.30, Thu, Fri 10–8.30; Great Court Mon–Wed, Sun 9–6, Thu–Sat 9am–11pm. Reading Room: daily 10–5.30, first Thu of month 10–8.30. Closed 24–26 Dec, 1 Jan, Good Fri

 Café (£), Restaurant (££)

Holborn, Tottenham Court Road, Russell Square

Regent Street 3, 6, 12, 13, 15, 88, 159; Piccadilly 9, 14, 19, 22, 38; New Bond Street southbound and Berkeley Street northbound 8

 Excellent. Access enquiries (020) 7323 8482; Artsline, voice and minicom (020) 7388 2227. Leaflet detailing facilities available at reception

Free

Highlights tour Daily 10.30, 1, 3. Eye Openers tours (free) hourly every day; pick up a leaflet for details

The Progress of Civilisation *is carved above the portico of the 'greatest jackdaw's nest in the world'*

The British Museum holds what is probably the greatest collection of antiquities in the world, and is also the country's most visited cultural attraction.

Founded in 1753 from the collection of Sir Hans Sloane—who bequeathed some 80,000 objects—the BM (as it is known to its regulars) has occupied its present site since 1823. The world's oldest museum has 4km (2.5 miles) of galleries displaying objects representing almost every aspect of international cultural history. Recent upheavals, however, which included the relocation of the British Library and the construction of a spectacular Great Court entrance, were as drastic as anything the museum has seen. The £100 million Great Court designed by Sir Norman Foster and opened to the public in December 2000, is Europe's largest covered square.

The following are just a few of the BM's greatest and most popular treasures. Pick up a floor plan to locate them: Starting on the ground floor, the sculptures from the Parthenon (the Elgin Marbles) are widely held to be the greatest works of their kind from ancient Greece. The

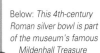

adjacent Nereid Monument, from Xanthos, Turkey, is a striking reconstructed temple. For more breathtaking sculptures on a monumental scale see the Assyrian human-headed winged bulls of Khorsabad. The museum boasts the greatest collection of Egyptology outside Cairo, including the famous Rosetta Stone, which enabled scholars to decipher the meaning of hieroglyphics. Not so renowned but equally worth while are the Oriental Collection (particularly the Indian sculptures) and the Mexican Gallery, both of which contain outstandingly beautiful works of art.

On the upper floors follow the crowds to the macabre Egyptian mummies and the preserved un-mummified body of 'Ginger'. In the Prehistoric and Romano-British sections, highlights include Lindow Man, the Sutton Hoo Treasure, the Mildenhall Treasure and the Lewis Chessmen. Close by, the Clocks and Watches collection, from the 16th to the 20th century, is one of the finest in the world. Be there on the hour when the clocks chime in unison. Easily overlooked among a welter of antiquities from Greece and Rome is the Portland Vase, a priceless example of the art of glass making.

Below: This 4th-century Roman silver bowl is part of the museum's famous Mildenhall Treasure

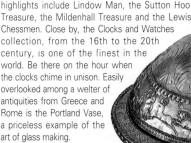

2
Covent Garden Piazza

🜚 29D3

🚇 Covent Garden

🍴 A wide choice (£–££) of cafés and restaurants

www.coventgardenmarket.co.uk

London's most continental square is thronged with shoppers and sightseers by day, and with theatregoers and revellers by night.

Covent Garden Piazza was laid out in the Italian style in 1630 by Inigo Jones. Initially it was a very fashionable address, but from 1670 onwards, with the advent of the main London fruit, flower and vegetable market, it was driven down-market and developed into a notorious red-light area. In 1830 its handsome centrepiece iron and glass hall was erected and the market continued trading at Covent Garden until 1974, when, finally defeated by transport logistics, it moved south of the river to Vauxhall. The site was then developed as a pedestrianized area, accommodating dozens of small shops and restaurants. The fruit and vegetable stalls were replaced by the Apple

Market, home to crafts, jewellery, clothing, accessories and antiques and collectables.

Today, only some arcading and St. Paul's Church remain of the original Piazza. By the church portico top-class buskers (licensed by the Covent Garden authorities) entertain large crowds daily. It was here, in 1662, that England's first ever Punch and Judy show was staged. St. Paul's is known as the Actors' Church because of the large number of memorials (and graves) of screen and stage stars it holds. It is well worth a look inside and its garden is a remarkably peaceful oasis amid the general hubbub.

The major museums around the Piazza are the London Transport Museum (▶ 54) and the Theatre Museum (▶ 71). For details of the Royal Opera House and the area's theatres (▶ 112–113).

Covent Garden's Central Market is now packed with fashionable shops and eateries

3

Houses of Parliament
(Palace of Westminster)

The home of the Mother of Parliaments and a masterpiece of Victorian Gothic, with over 1,000 rooms and the world's most famous clock tower.

The Houses of Parliament, seat of British government, dates back to *c*1050, when William the Conqueror built his Palace of Westminster on this site. It evolved into a parliament around the mid-13th century and continued to be used as a royal palace until 1512, when Henry VIII moved his court to Whitehall. In 1834 a disastrous fire burned everything above ground (with the exception of Westminster Hall, the cloisters and the Jewel Tower), and so construction began of the building that you see today. The principal architect was Charles Barry, though the flamboyant ubiquitous Gothic decorative touches are the work of his assistant, Augustus Pugin. By 1860, some 20 years later than planned and around £1.4 million over budget, it was virtually complete. The best-known part of the Houses is the clock tower, referred to as Big Ben—though to be precise this is the name of the great 13-ton bell that chimes every hour. After dark a light above the clock face indicates when Parliament is 'sitting' (when it is in session).

The modern Houses of Parliament divide principally into two debating chambers. The House of Commons comprises Members of Parliament (MPs) who are the elected representatives of the British people. Their functions are legislation and (as opposition) government scrutiny. The non-elected House of Lords is an apolitical body of the great and good, who examine proposed legislation from the Commons and also act as the highest Appeal Court in the land.

✝ 29D3

✉ Public entrance on St. Margaret Street

☎ Information Office (020) 7219 4272 (Commons), (020) 7219 3107 (Lords); www.parliament.uk

🕐 The public may attend debates in both Houses

Ⓔ Westminster

🚌 3, 11, 12, 24, 77a, 211

🚆 Waterloo

♿ For access ☎ (020) 7219 3003

✋ Free

Richard I ('the Lionheart'), the heroic English crusader king, in Old Palace Yard outside Parliament

4
National Gallery

29D3

Trafalgar Square

(020) 7747 2885;
www.national
gallery.org.uk

Daily 10–6 (Wed until 9).
Closed 24–26 Dec, 1
Jan

Café (£), Brasserie (££)

Charing Cross, Leicester
Square

3, 6, 9, 11, 12, 13, 15,
23, 24, 29, 53, 77a, 88,
91, 139, 159, 176, 453

Charing Cross

Lower Regent Street

Excellent

Free

Home to one of the finest and most comprehensive collections of Western art in the world, the National Gallery houses over 2,000 paintings.

The collection is divided chronologically, with the Sainsbury Wing housing the oldest paintings, from 1260 to 1510. Two of the most famous works are *The Virgin and Child* cartoon by Leonardo da Vinci and *Venus and Mars* by Botticelli. *The Doge* by Giovanni Bellini is considered the greatest-ever Venetian portrait. Less famous but equally worth while are *The Wilton Diptych* (by an unknown artist), *The Battle of San Romano* by Uccello, *The Baptism of Christ* by Piero della Francesca and *The Arnolfini Portrait* by Jan van Eyck.

The West Wing progresses to 1600 and includes *The Entombment* (unfinished) by Michelangelo. Two famous mythology paintings are *Bacchus and Ariadne* by Titian and *Allegory with Venus and Cupid* by Bronzino. More 'worldly' masterpieces include Holbein's *Ambassadors* and *Pope Julius II* by Raphael.

The North Wing deals with the 17th century. Among its 15 or so Rembrandts is the sorrowful *Self Portrait at the Age of 63* (that same year he died a pauper). Contrast this with the pompous *Equestrian Portrait of Charles I* by Van Dyck, and the charming *Le Chapeau de Paille* (Straw Hat) portrait by Rubens. *Young Woman Standing at a Virginal* by Vermeer, *The Rokeby Venus* by Velázquez and *Enchanted Castle* by Claude are also worth seeking out.

The East Wing (1700–1900) contains a whole host of popular favourites: *Sunflowers* by Van Gogh; *Bathers at Asnières* by Seurat; *Gare St-Lazare* by Monet; and from the British school, *Hay-Wain* by Constable and *Fighting Temeraire* by J. M. W. Turner.

The National Gallery houses the country's most popular art collection, attracting almost 5 million visitors per year

5
Natural History Museum

A family favourite where dinosaurs roar back to life, an earthquake shakes the ground and creepy-crawlies make the flesh tingle.

Moving with the times: animatronic meat-eaters in Kensington

To thousands of children the Natural History Museum is 'the Dinosaur Museum', and no visit would be complete without poring over the superbly displayed skeletons of the museum's world-famous collection. There's much more here than just prehistoric monsters, however. Highest of all on the heavyweights list is the blue whale. It may only be a model, but what a model, measuring over 28m (30.5ft) with a real 25m (27ft) skeleton alongside. Around here there is a vast array of mammal specimens to ponder on while at the other end of the size spectrum, children (if not adults) will love the 'Creepy-crawlies' exhibition. For more ethereal concepts, visit the state-of-the-art Ecology display and gingerly examine the workings of your own body in the Human biology section. One of the museum's greatest attractions is its very structure, built in neo-Gothic cathedral style by Alfred Waterhouse in 1880. The Cromwell Road frontage is magnificent and there is a wealth of interior detail to enjoy.

Once you've seen life on earth, explore the adjacent Earth Galleries (formerly known as the Geological Museum) which tell the story of the earth's formation and its on-going upheavals. This is a far cry from the old museum's displays of rocks in dusty glass cases, though its collection of gemstones remains a highlight. The main attraction is The Power Within exhibitions where the ground-shaking sensations of a real earthquake are simulated and audio visuals show breathtaking footage of volcanoes and their devastating effects on everyday objects.

✚ 28A1

✉ Cromwell Road (Life Galleries), Exhibition Road (Earth Galleries)

☎ (020) 7942 5000; (020) 7942 5011 Sat and Sun; www.nhm.ac.uk

🕐 Mon–Sat 10–5.50, Sun and public hols 11–5.50

🍴 Life Galleries Restaurant (££); Waterhouse Café (£); Globe Café (£)

Ⓓ South Kensington

🚌 74

♿ Excellent

✋ Free

❓ Tours: Wildlife Garden Apr–Oct 12–5 (45 min). Book at Life Galleries information desk (inexpensive). Darwin Centre tours, book on arrival (free)

6
St. Paul's Cathedral

✝ 29E3

✉ St. Paul's Churchyard

☎ (020) 7236 4128;
www.stpauls.co.uk

🕐 Mon–Sat 8.30–4.30 (last admission 4)

🍴 Refectory Restaurant (£); Café in crypt (£)

🚇 St. Paul's

🚌 11, 15, 17, 23, 26

🚉 Cannon Street

♿ Floor and crypt excellent. Galleries inaccessible

✋ Expensive

❓ Self-guided audio tours, 90-min guided tours

The Mother Church of the Diocese of London and the supreme work of Sir Christopher Wren, one of the world's great architects.

Work began on the present St. Paul's Cathedral after the Great Fire of 1666 had destroyed its predecessor, Old St. Paul's. Its foundation stone was laid by Christopher Wren in 1675 and after 35 years of sweat and toil (during which time Wren's salary was halved as punishment for slow progress) it was completed in 1710. Take time to enjoy the magnificent west front before entering the church. Inside it is surprisingly light and airy, largely as a result of the use of plain glass windows (much favoured by Wren), which were installed to replace the old stained glass destroyed during World War II.

Go past the huge monument to the Duke of Wellington and stop in the middle of the transepts to look skywards to the wonderful dome—one of the three largest in the world. Move on to the choir, the most lavishly decorated part of the church, and don't miss the scorch-marked statue of John Donne (poet and Dean of Old St. Paul's). This is one of London's very few monuments to survive the Great Fire of 1666.

Descend to the crypt, where you will find the tombs of some of Britain's greatest heroes, including the Duke of Wellington and Lord Nelson, and, of course, Christopher Wren himself. Return to the church and begin the ascent to the galleries. The justifiably famous Whispering Gallery, whose remarkable acoustics will carry a whisper quite audibly from one side to the other, is perched 30m (98ft) above the floor. Finally, after a total of 530 steps, you will reach the Golden Gallery, where you will be rewarded with one of the finest views in all London. Return to the cathedral floor and contemplate William Holman Hunt's uplifting masterpiece, *The Light of the World.*

Don't miss St. Paul's by night, when it is dramatically floodlit

7
Science Museum

Don't be put off by the name or the concept of a museum of science. This is an exhibition of how things work and how technology has evolved.

The Science Museum is one of the world's finest collections of its kind. It is a huge undertaking, however, and you can't hope to see and understand everything here in a single visit. On the other hand there are so many pieces that are landmarks of industrial history, technological milestones, works of art, or just amazing objects in their own right, there really is something that everyone can identify with and admire.

To see the best of the collection in one visit buy the excellent museum guidebook, which will navigate you through the 'must-see' exhibits such as Stephenson's *Rocket*, Edison's early lamps, the ill-fated Ford Edsel motorcar, the prototype computer (the dauntingly huge Babbage's Difference Engine), the Apollo 10 Command module, the first iron lung, ancient orreries, and many other famous technological landmarks.

The Science Museum is famous for its pioneering interactive hands-on areas and adults with children should start down in the basement, then progress to Launch Pad. Here youngsters can discover how machines and gadgets work. Other family favourites include the Flight Galleries, featuring a whole array of historic aircraft, many of them slung dramatically from the ceiling. For sheer spectacle it's hard to beat the East Hall, where some of the great beam-and-steam behemoths that powered the Industrial Revolution still push and thrust their mighty workings.

If you have any energy left, the Wellcome History of Medicine on the top floor is a fascinating collection with an emphasis on ancient and tribal medicines, and features some blood-curdling practices.

 28A2

Exhibition Road

(020) 7942 4455/0870 870 4868; www.science museum.org.uk

Daily 10–6. Closed 24–26 Dec

Museum restaurant (£), cafés (£), picnic areas

South Kensington

 74, 9, 10, 14, 49, 52, 70, 345, 360, 414, C1

 Excellent

Free

IMAX cinema (expensive); simulators (inexpensive–moderate)

Stephenson's Rocket *is a Science Museum favourite*

8

Tower of London

 29F3

✉ Tower of London

☎ 0870) 756 6060;
www.hrp.org.uk

🕐 Mar–Oct Tue–Sat 9–6,
Sun, Mon 10–6 (last
admission 5); Nov–Feb
Tue–Sat 9–5, Sun–Mon
10–5 (last admission 4)

🍴 Café (£), restaurant (£)

Ⓣ Tower Hill

🚌 15, 25, 42, 78, 100, D1

🚆 Fenchurch Street,
London Bridge

♿ Tower staff very willing
to help but inherent
problems with old
buildings. Phone in
advance for details

✋ Very expensive

❓ Buy tickets in advance
online or from any
underground station to
avoid waiting at the
Tower entrance

*London's foremost historical site, the Tower has
served as castle, palace, prison, arsenal, jewel house
and site of execution over its 900-year lifespan.*

The oldest part of the Tower of London is the great central
keep. Known as the White Tower, it was begun by
William I in 1078 to intimidate his newly conquered
subjects; the rest of the fortifications took on their present
shape in the late 13th and early 14th centuries.

All tours begin with an hour long, highly entertaining
guided walk led by one of the Tower's traditionally dressed
Yeoman Warders (Beefeaters). They gleefully relate stories
of imprisonment, torture and intrigue—later on you can
check out the Torture in the Tower exhibition for further
gruesome details—while taking you past a few of the 20
towers, the famous ravens ('only so long as they stay will
the White Tower stand'), Traitors' Gate and the execution
site of Tower Green. Here, among others, Henry VIII's
wives Anne Boleyn and Catherine Howard lost their heads.
After visiting the adjacent Chapel of St. Peter ad Vincula
you are left to explore by yourself and join the inevitable
queues at the Jewel House and the White Tower. Both are
well worth the wait. The former houses the Crown
Jewels, many of which date back to the 17th-century
Restoration period and are still used by the present Queen
and royal family. The White Tower is home to the beautiful
11th-century Chapel of St. John. Also highly recommended
is a visit to the restored rooms of the medieval palace.

9

Victoria & Albert Museum

The V&A is not only Britain's national museum of art and design, but comprises the greatest collection of decorative arts in the world.

The V&A was founded in 1852 with the objective of exhibiting the world's very best examples of design and applied arts in order to inspire students and crafts people. It has subsequently grown to include an astonishing and immense diversity of objects. Your first task is to arm yourself with a map and index to help you navigate the 13km (8 miles) labyrinth of stairs and corridors.

Perhaps the V&A's greatest treasures are the Raphael Cartoons, seven huge tapestry designs that have become even more famous than the actual tapestries themselves (which hang in the Sistine Chapel in Rome). While on the ground floor, don't miss the Italian Renaissance sculptures; the Cast Courts, full-size plaster casts of fascinating European masterpieces including Trajan's Column and Michelangelo's *David*; and the Morris, Poynter and Gamble Rooms, the V&A's original refreshment rooms and masterpieces of Victorian decoration. Dip into the multifarious treasures of the Orient from China, Japan, Islam and India—don't miss Tipoo's Tiger, one of the museum's most famous pieces—and the Fashion collections.

Look for the Glass Gallery, a wonderful exhibition of glass spanning a period of 4,000 years. See the lavishly refurbished British Galleries and the Silver galleries, a culmination of an eight-year V&A project, and tucked away in the Paintings galleries are some of John Constable's best works.

 28A2

 Entrances on Exhibition Road, Cromwell Road

 (020) 7942 2000; 0870 442 0808 for recorded information; www.vam.ac.uk

 Daily 10–5.45. Wed and last Fri of month 10–10. Closed 24–26, 31 Dec, 1 Jan

 Excellent cafés (£) and restaurant (££) on premises

 South Kensington

 C1, 14, 74 stop outside Cromwell Road entrance

 Excellent. Pick up a detailed leaflet from information desk

Free

Tours: introductory tours daily (lasting 1 hour) half hourly 10.30–3.30; also Wed 4.30, 7.30

Left: *The V&A was opened by Queen Victoria in 1857; the central tower is modelled on an imperial crown*
Opposite: *The Tower of London protects the Crown Jewels*

10
Westminster Abbey

✝ 29D2

✉ Dean's Yard, Broad Sanctuary

☎ Abbey (020) 7654 4900; www.westminster-abbey.org

🕐 Nave, cloisters daily 8–6; abbey Mon–Fri 9.30–4.45 (Wed 9.30–7), Sat 9–2.45. Last admission 1 hour before closing time. No sightseeing on Sun; Pyx Chamber, Chapter House and museum daily 10.30–4

🍴 Coffee stands outside abbey and in cloister

Ⓜ Westminster, St James's Park

🚌 3, 11, 24, 53, 77a, 159, 211

♿ Ramped wheelchair access available

✋ Cloisters free; abbey expensive, includes Chapter House, museum, Pyx Chamber

❓ Guided tours: Apr–Sep Mon–Fri 10, 10.30, 11, 2, 2.30, 3; Sat 10.30, 11, 12.30; Oct–Mar Mon–Fri 10, 11, 2, 2.30; Sat 10, 10.30, 11. ☎ Reserve tours in advance (020) 7654 4900 ✋ Moderate; Audio tour available ✋ Inexpensive–moderate. College Garden 🕐 Apr–Sep Tue–Thu 10–6; rest of year 10–4. Band concert Wed ✋ Free

An ornate pulpit among Westminster Abbey's soaring arches

The coronation site of British royalty, the last resting place of kings, queens and celebrities, this architectural triumph is awash with history.

Westminster Abbey was founded *c*1050 by Edward the Confessor who was the first king to be buried here. William the Conqueror was crowned king in the abbey on Christmas Day in 1066 and so began a tradition that was last re-enacted in 1953 when the coronation of the present monarch, Queen Elizabeth II, took place here.

The present building dates mostly from the 13th century and the reign of Henry III. The nave is chock-a-block with graves and monuments, none more famous than the Tomb of the Unknown Warrior who represents the 765,000 British servicemen killed in World War I, though the real glory of the abbey lies beyond the sumptuously carved and gilded screen (by which Isaac Newton and Charles Darwin lie) in the Royal Chapels. Here you will find the coronation chair and the often-magnificent tombs of dozens of royals. The abbey's *tour de force* lies at its easternmost point; Henry VII's Chapel, built between 1503 and 1519, with its sublime fan-vaulting. In the south transept is the famous Poets' Corner where many celebrated writers, musicians and artists are honoured.

Try to see the beautiful abbey precinct that includes the cloisters, the Chapter House, the Westminster Abbey Museum (with contemporary royal wax effigies) and the Pyx ('money chest') Chamber (closed at time of writing).

What to See

Central London   31–77
In the Know   52–53
Food and Drink   60–61
Outer London and
 Beyond   79–90

Above: *Detail in Pall Mall*
Right: *Letter box*

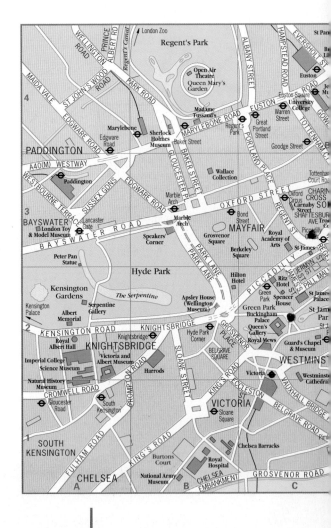

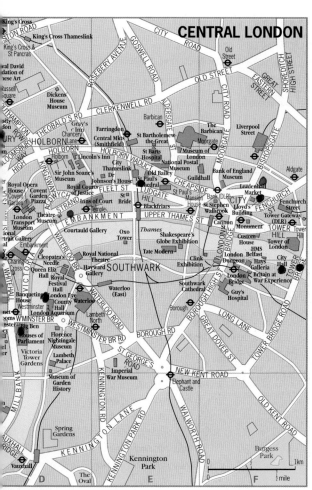

CENTRAL LONDON

King's Cross
KSTON ROAD
King's Cross Thameslink
King's Cross &
St Pancras
val David
dation of
nese Art
Russell
Square
THAMPTON
sity
ion
Dickens'
House
Museum
BURY
THEOBALD'S RD
Gray's
Inn
CLERKENWELL RD
Barbican
OLD STREET
Old
Street
CITY
ROAD
GOSWELL ROAD
ROSEBERY AVENUE
ADERSGATE
CITY ROAD
GREAT
EASTERN
STREET
SHOREDITCH
HIGH STREET
HOLBORN
Chancery
Lane
Farringdon
Central Mkts
(Smithfield)
The
Barbican
Liverpool
Street
BISHOPSGATE
Aldgate
HOLBORN
HIGH
Lincoln's Inn
HOLBORN VIADUCT
St Bartholomew
the Great
Moorgate
KINGSWAY
BLOOMSBURY
WAY
Sir John Soane's
Museum
City
Thameslink
Dr
Johnson's House
St Barts
Hospital
Old Bailey
Museum of
London
National Postal
Museum
Bank of England
Museum
Leadenhall
Market
Royal Opera
House
Covent
Garden
Covent
Garden
Piazza
Royal Courts
of Justice
FLEET ST
St
Bride
St Paul's
Cathedral
LUDGATE
HILL
CHEAPSIDE
St Paul's
Guildhall
Bank (DLR)
CITY
Mansion
House
St Stephen
Walbrook
Lloyd's
Building
FENCHURCH
Fenchurch
Street
London
Transport
Museum
STRAND
ALDWYCH
Temple
Inns of Court
Blackfriars
UPPER THAMES ST
Cannon
Street
Monument
Custom
House
TOWER
Tower Gateway
(DLR)
HILL
TOWER
Tower
Hill
Theatre
Museum
EMBANKMENT
Courtauld Gallery
Oxo
Tower
Thames
Shakespeare's
Globe Exhibition
Tate Modern
Clink
Exhibition
London
Dungeon
HMS Belfast
Hays
Galleria
Britain at
War Experience
Tower of
London
ional
trait Gallery
Embankment
Cleopatra's
Needle
Royal National
Theatre
Hayward
Gallery
SOUTHWARK
Charing
Cross
WHITEHALL
Queen Eliz
Hall
Royal
Festival
Hall
Waterloo
(East)
London
Bridge
Southwark
Cathedral
City
Hall
WATERLOO BRIDGE
London Eye
County
Hall
London Aquarium
Waterloo
Borough
Guy's
Hospital
LONG LANE
TOWER BRIDGE ROAD
Banqueting
House
Westminster
net
oms
ister
W'MINSTER BR
Big Ben
Houses of
Parliament
Victoria
Tower
Gardens
WESTMINSTER BR RD
Lambeth
North
VICTORIA
BOROUGH RD
Lambeth
Palace
Florence
Nightingale
Museum
BOROUGH HIGH ST
GREAT DOVER ST
ST GEORGE'S
ROAD
NEW KENT ROAD
Elephant and
Castle
OLD KENT ROAD
MILLBANK
Museum of
Garden
History
Imperial
War Museum
KENNINGTON RD
KENNINGTON LANE
KENNINGTON PARK RD
WALWORTH ROAD
AUXHALL
RIDGE
Spring
Gardens
KENNINGTON ROAD
Kennington
Park
Burgess
Park
Vauxhall

D
The
Oval
E
Kennington
Park
F

1km
½ mile

-Somerset house

London

London is one of the world's few truly great cities. Its depth of history is unrivalled by any other major capital, its shopping is the envy of Europe, and it is currently undergoing a renaissance in cuisine and fashion. With around 27 million visitors per year and one of the world's most cosmopolitan indigenous make-ups, it is a global melting pot, catering for all tastes and nationalities.

Of course, not all is perfect. Hotel prices are too high, the weather is unpredictable (so be prepared!) and the traffic can be horrendous. On the other hand, London is a very civilized city. Life may be fast and sometimes impersonal, but it is very rarely aggressive, and oases of calm—the parks, historic churches, museums, and hotels and department stores serving afternoon tea—are never more than a few steps away.

> *' Why, Sir, you find no man at all intellectual who is willing to leave London. No, Sir, when a man is tired of London, he is tired of life; for there is in London all that life can afford. '*

DR SAMUEL JOHNSON, (1777)

Central London

One of the questions asked by many first-time visitors to London is 'Where is the centre?' The simple answer is that as London has evolved from a series of villages it has many centres. However, the West End—a rather vague geographical term generally covering Piccadilly, Soho and Covent Garden—is the accepted hub of the city for shopping, eating, drinking and nightlife, as well as a good slice of sightseeing.

Trafalgar Square is the exact centre of London, from which all distances are measured

For orientation purposes Trafalgar Square, with its landmark Nelson's Column, is a good place to start. To the north is the West End, and beyond that Bloomsbury, a leafy district of handsome squares and home of the British Museum. Due west from Trafalgar Square is Westminster and Whitehall, the hub of government, from where a short walk across St. James's Park leads to Buckingham Palace. Further west is Kensington and Hyde Park. Just north of the park is a popular hotel location, while to the south lie three of London's world-famous museums. A little further southwest is fashionable Chelsea.

Due east from Trafalgar Square, past Covent Garden, is the original City of London. This is both London's modern financial district and its ancient heart, where Roman walls butt up against skyscraping offices. Most visitors venture no farther east than the Tower of London, but beyond here the new Docklands area is extending the sightseeing range. Finally, don't forget the south bank of the river, where the new Riverside Walk stretches from the South Bank Arts Centre to historic Southwark.

31

Below: *BA's London Eye*

+ 28B2
✉ 149 Piccadilly, Hyde Park Corner
☎ (020) 7499 5676; www.english-heritage.org.uk
🕐 Tue–Sun 10–5 (last admission 4.30). Closed Mon (open public hol Mon except May Day), Good Fri, 24–26 Dec, 1 Jan
🍴 The Grenadier (£)
🚇 Hyde Park Corner
♿ Limited access due to steps
💷 Moderate. Free on Waterloo Day (18 Jun)

+ 29F
✉ Bartholomew Lane
☎ (020) 7601 5545; www.bankofengland.co.uk/museum
🍴 Mon–Fri 10–5
🍴 Sweetings (££) (➤ 96)
🚇 Bank
♿ Excellent
💷 Free

What to See in Central London

APSLEY HOUSE ✪✪

Apsley House, also known as the Wellington Museum, was the London home of Arthur Wellesley, first Duke of Wellington, from 1829 until his death in 1852. Wellington was the greatest soldier of his day, achieving major military successes in India, Spain and Portugal before crowning his career with the defeat of Napoleon at Waterloo in 1815.

The museum divides into two parts. Collections of plate and china, magnificent table centrepieces, swords, medals and so on relate to the Duke's adventures, and there is also an outstanding picture collection with works by many famous old masters. Intriguingly, the most memorable piece is a heroic oversized statue of Napoleon by Canova (commissioned by the Little Emperor himself) in which he is depicted as a god.

BANK OF ENGLAND MUSEUM ✪

The story of Britain's monetary and banking system since 1604 is told at this museum. The Bank of England is the nation's central bank, functioning at the heart of one of the world's largest and most sophisicated financial centres. A visit to this small but lively museum will enlighten you as to its workings and its history. Having been in existence so long, the bank has accumulated a considerable number of items associated with its history. The collections include banknotes and coins, furniture, books, pictures and statues. Highlights are its real gold bullion (each house-brick-sized bar is worth around £70,000), the reproduction banking hall and the award-winning interactive screens and currency dealing computer game.

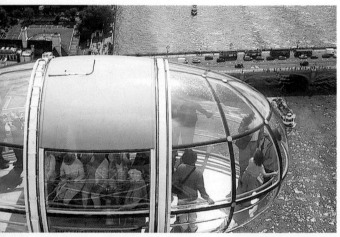

BANQUETING HOUSE ⭐

The Banqueting House is the only surviving part of Henry VIII's great Whitehall Palace, which burned down in 1698. Designed in classical style by Inigo Jones, it was completed in 1622 and is famous for its magnificent ceiling painting by Rubens. This huge work was commissioned by Charles I to celebrate the wisdom of the reign of the Stuart dynasty and depicts his father, James I. It was therefore to provide an ironic backdrop to the events of 30 January 1649 when Charles, defeated in the English Civil War, stepped out from a window of the Banqueting House on to a scaffold to face the executioner's axe.

The vaulted undercroft, formerly the wine cellar of James I, is also open to the public.

🟫 29D2
✉ Whitehall
☎ 0870 751 5178;
  www.hrp.org.uk
🕐 Mon–Sat 10–5. Closed
  24–26 Dec, 1 Jan, Good
  Fri, all public hols and for
  functions at short notice
🍴 Café-in-the-Crypt, St.
  Martin-in-the-Fields,
  Trafalgar Square (£)
  (➤ 92)
🚇 Westminster,
  Embankment
♿ Only undercroft
  accessible
🎫 Moderate

BRITISH MUSEUM (➤ 16–17, TOP TEN)

BRITISH AIRWAYS LONDON EYE ⭐⭐⭐

This giant landmark wheel was erected as part of the capital's Millennium celebrations and has quickly become one of the hottest attraction tickets in town. Its 32 observation capsules soar majestically 135m (443ft) directly above the Thames, making it the tallest wheel of its kind in the world. A full revolution takes 30 minutes, offering magnificent views right across the heart of central London and far beyond.

A limited number of seats are available to personal callers (these are quickly snapped up), the rest are reserved by telephone. The best advice is to reserve well ahead so as not to miss out. Even with a ticket, however, boarding takes around 30 minutes.

🟫 29D2
✉ Jubilee Gardens
☎ 0870 990 8881; booking
  0870 500 0600;
  www.ba-londoneye.com
🕐 Daily May, Jun, Sep
  9.30am–9pm; Jul–Aug
  9.30am–10pm; Oct–Dec,
  Feb–Apr 9.30–8 (times
  may vary)
🚇 Waterloo
♿ Excellent 🎫 Expensive

Above: *Opulent styling in the Banqueting House*

✚ 28C2
✉ The Mall
☎ (020) 7766 7324;
www.royal.gov.uk

State Rooms
✉ Buckingham Palace
🕐 Tours daily Aug–Sep
9.30–4.15 (last tour)
🚇 Green Park, Hyde Park
Corner, St James's Park,
Victoria
♿ Excellent
🍴 Very expensive
🎫 Tickets from Green Park
office on day of visit or in
advance by credit card
☎ (020) 7766 7300

Royal Mews
✉ Buckingham Palace Road
🕐 Mar–late Jul, Oct,
Sat–Thu 11–4 (last
admission 3.15); late
Jul–Sep daily 10–5 (last
admission 4.15)
🚇 Hyde Park Corner, St.
James's Park, Victoria
♿ Excellent 🍴 Moderate

Queen's Gallery
✉ Buckingham Palace Road
🕐 Daily 10–5.30 (last
admission 4.30)
♿ Excellent 🍴 Expensive

Above: *Queen Victoria
Memorial and
Buckingham Palace*

BUCKINGHAM PALACE ✪✪✪

World-famous as the London home of the Queen, this vast, sprawling, 600-room house was built mostly between 1820 and 1837, although the familiar East Front public face of the palace was not added until 1913. Buckingham Palace has been opening its doors to the public since 1993, with proceeds going towards the restoration of Windsor Castle (▶ 90). Visitors get to view the **State Rooms**, which are furnished with some of the most important works of art from the Royal Collection (including pictures by Van Dyck, Rembrandt and Rubens)—one of the largest and most valuable private art collections in the world. There's no chance of spotting any of the royal family, however, as they are always away at another of the royal residences when the palace is open.

Around the corner, on Buckingham Palace Road is the **Queen's Gallery**, which reopened for the Queen's Gold Jubilee in 2002 and exhibits items from the Royal Collection. Alongside is the **Royal Mews**, where, among the horses and tack, is a display of the opulent carriages that are wheeled out on state occasions.

The Changing of the Guard is still the most popular reason for visiting the palace. It takes place daily from April to July and on alternate days the rest of the year (wet weather permitting). At around 11.15 the St James's Palace part of the old guard marches down the Mall to meet the old guard of Buckingham Palace. There they await the arrival, at 11.30, of the new guard from Wellington Barracks who are accompanied by a band. Keys are ceremonially handed from the old to the new guard while the band plays. When the sentries have been changed, at around 12.05, the old guard return to Wellington Barracks and the new part of the St James's Palace guard march off to St James's Palace. As it can be extremely busy, aim to get close to the railings well before 11.00, particularly in high summer.

CABINET WAR ROOMS AND CHURCHILL MUSEUM ✪✪

This underground warren of rooms provided secure accommodation for the War Cabinet and their military advisers during World War II and was used on over 100 occasions. Today it is a time capsule, with the clocks stopped at 16.58 on 15 October 1940 and the ghost of Winston Churchill hanging heavy in the stuffy air. You can view his private kitchen, dining room and Mrs Churchill's bedroom. Many of his stirring speeches were made from here and some of these are played to heighten the evocative atmosphere.

CHELSEA ✪✪✪

One of London's most fashionable suburbs in every sense, Chelsea was synonymous with both London's 'Swinging 60s' and the late 1970s punk rock movement. The latter was in fact born here, just off the famous King's Road. Today it is more classy though still very lively. The area is best explored on foot (► 36).

➕ 29D2
✉ Clive Steps, King Charles Street
☎ (020) 7930 6961; www.iwm.org.uk
🕐 Daily 9.30–6 (last admission 5.15)
🚇 Westminster
♿ Excellent
💷 Expensive (under 16 free)
❓ Admission includes audio guide

➕ 28A1

Chelsea's famous pink Albert Bridge is the prettiest of all the Thames crossings

Around Chelsea

Distance
5–6km (3–3.75 miles)

Time
2–6 hours depending on visits

Start point
🚇 Sloane Square
✚ 28B1

End point
🚇 Sloane Square
✚ 28B1

Lunch
Pizza Express (£)
✉ 152 King's Road
☎ (020) 7351 5031

Royal Hospital, Chelsea
☎ (020) 7881 5303
🕐 Mon–Fri 10–12, 2–4, Sat 2–4; (also Sun 2–4, May–Sep only)
🖐 Free, donations welcome

Chelsea Physic Garden
☎ (020) 7352 5646
🕐 Early Apr to late Oct Wed 12–5, Sun 2–6
🖐 Moderate

Start from Sloane Square underground station and walk straight ahead, down the King's Road, with Sloane Square and its statue of Sir Hans Sloane on your right.

About 100m (110 yards) past the square turn left into Cheltenham Terrace with the Duke of York's (Territorial Army) Headquarters to your left. Turn right on to St. Leonard's Terrace, former home of Bram Stoker (the creator of Dracula), with the green fields of Burton Court to your left.

The building on the other side of the fields is the Royal Hospital, home to the famous Chelsea pensioners.

Turn right into Royal Hospital Road (or left to visit the Hospital), passing the National Army Museum (▶ 59). Turn right into Tite Street, which includes such famous former residents as Oscar Wilde (No 34), John Singer Sargent (No. 31) and Augustus John (No. 33). Turn right into Dilke Street, catching a glimpse through the side gate of the Chelsea Physic Garden.

Physic simply means 'of things natural'. This is the second-oldest botanic garden in the country, founded in 1673.

Turn left into Swan Walk past the Physic Garden entrance, then right on to Cheyne Walk.

This handsome terrace was also home to some of Chelsea's famous artists and writers including George Eliot (No 4) and Dante Gabrielle Rossetti (No. 16).

Continue along the Embankment, past pretty pink Albert Bridge, to Chelsea Old Church.

A statue of Sir Thomas More sits outside the church and his intended tomb, inside, is occupied by his wife.

Turn right into Church Street until you rejoin the shops of King's Road, then turn right to return to Sloane Square.

CLINK PRISON MUSEUM ✪

From the early 16th century until 1780, the Clink, 'a very dismal hole', was the jail of the Bishops of Winchester, used to incarcerate the lowlife of Bankside—including prostitutes, drunks, debtors, and actors who had 'broken the peace'. In fact it was so notorious that it entered the English language as a synonym for jail. Not that the bishop held the moral high ground. He acted effectively as protection racketeer and pimp, licensing, and profiting from, the various illegal activities that went on in the badlands of Bankside. You can learn all about these times at the Clink Prison Museum. Alongside part of a wall with a great rose window is all that survives of the Bishops Palace, Winchester House, built in 1109.

🏠 293F
✉ 1 Clink Street
☎ (020) 7403 0900
🕐 Jul–Sep daily 10–9; Oct–Jun Mon–Fri 10–6, Sat, Sun 10–7.30
🍴 fish!, Cathedral Street, Borough Market (££)
🚇 London Bridge (10-minute walk)
♿ None
💷 Moderate

Opposite page: *Sculpture of Thomas More at Chelsea Old Church*
Left: *It's not the quantity but the quality that counts at Courtauld Gallery*

COURTAULD GALLERY ✪✪✪

The Courtauld Gallery has been called the greatest concentration of Western European art anywhere in the world and features a great collection of Impressionist paintings. It is housed in Somerset House, one of the finest and most important 18th-century public buildings in London.

The Impressionists and Post-Impressionists are top priority, particularly Van Gogh's *Self Portrait with Bandaged Ear* and Manet's *Bar at the Folies Bergère*. Other paintings include *Le Déjeuner sur l'Herbe*, also by Manet, *The Card Players* by Cézanne, *La Loge* by Renoir, *Two Dancers on a Stage* by Degas and Gauguin's Tahitian works. The collection goes back to the 15th century, and early masterpieces include works by Cranach the Elder, a superb Holy Trinity by Botticelli and from the early 17th century a large number of paintings by Rubens. There are also some fine 20th-century works.

🏠 29D3
✉ Somerset House, Strand
☎ (020) 7848 2526; www.courtauld.ac.uk/gallery
🕐 Daily 10–6
🍴 Café (£), Admiralty restaurnt (£££)
🚇 Temple (closed Sun), Covent Garden, Holborn
♿ Excellent
💷 Moderate; children free. Free Mon 10–2 (except public hols)

COVENT GARDEN PIAZZA (▶ 18, TOP TEN)

Around Covent Garden

Distance
3–4km (2.5 miles)

Time
1 hour without stops

Start point
🚇 Leicester Square
✚ 29D3

End point
🚇 Covent Garden
✚ 29D3

Lunch
World Food Café
✉ Neal's Yard (£)
☎ (020) 7379 0298

The Neal's Yard water clock is typical of Covent Garden's creative and fun mood

This walk can take all day if the shops and cafés along the way prove irresistible.

> *Leave Leicester Square underground station via a Charing Cross Road exit and walk a short way in the direction of Trafalgar Square. Turn left into Cecil Court.*

While away some time here in one of London's popular book-browsing alleyways, with individual small shops.

> *At the top, cross St. Martin's Lane and enter the tiny gas-lit alleyway marked Goodwin's Court (look for the two pubs, the Angel and Crown and the Green Man and French Horn, the alley is in-between).*

This is the oldest residential part of Covent Garden, with beautiful 18th-century bow-windowed houses.

> *Turn left into Bedfordbury, then almost immediately right into New Row, a charming pedestrianized street with many excellent small shops. Continue up New Row to King Street, pausing to admire No. 43, built in 1717, which is one of the oldest and most attractive buildings.*

Almost opposite here is one of the entrances to St. Paul's Church (► 18).

> *Keep the Piazza and central market area (► 18) on your right and turn left into James Street, past Covent Garden underground station. Cross Long Acre into Neal Street, another of Covent Garden's characteristic pedestrianized shopping streets. Turn left into Short's Gardens, then, by the splendid water clock on top of the Neal's Yard Wholefood Warehouse, turn right into Neal's Yard.*

This delightfully pretty courtyard festooned with window boxes is a wholefood haven, full of vegetarian cafés and restaurants.

> *Retrace your steps back to Covent Garden underground station.*

DESIGN MUSEUM ✪✪

The Design Museum was set up in 1989 as the brainchild of Britain's leading design and style guru, Sir Terence Conran. Its aim is to promote an awareness of the importance of design and the contribution it makes to everyday life, particularly when related to mass-produced objects. Although this may not sound particularly promising (and the severe lines of its brilliant white Bauhaus building hardly provide reassurance to the casual visitor), it is well worth a visit. The collection divides broadly into two parts. The more conventional historic part shows the design evolution of familiar workaday items, such as domestic appliances, cameras and cars. The upper Review Gallery is an intriguing fly-on-the-wall showcase for the very latest ideas; some currently in production, some at prototype stage, others stuck permanently on the drawing board. Interactive computer stations cater for a new generation of would-be designers.

- ✚ 81D3
- ✉ Butler's Wharf, Shad Thames
- ☎ 0870 833 9955; 0870 909 9009; www.designmuseum.org
- 🕐 Daily 10–5.45, (Fri 10–9). Closed 25–26 Dec
- 🍴 Blueprint Café restaurant (££), café (£)
- Ⓔ London Bridge, Tower Hill
- ♿ Excellent
- 🎟 Moderate

DICKENS HOUSE MUSEUM ✪✪

Dating from 1801, this smart middle-class residence is the only surviving house in which Charles Dickens lived for any length of time while in London. He stayed here from April 1837 to December 1839, long enough to secure his burgeoning reputation by writing the final instalments of *The Pickwick Papers*, almost all of *Oliver Twist*, the whole of *Nicholas Nickleby* and the start of *Barnaby Rudge*. Opened as a museum in 1925, the house now holds the finest collection of Dickens memorabilia in existence, with many of the exhibits reflecting the novels that were written here.

- ✚ 29D4
- ✉ 48 Doughty Street
- ☎ (020) 7405 2127; www.dickensmuseum.com
- 🕐 Mon–Sat 10–5, Sun 11–5 (last admission 4.30)
- 🍴 The Lamb pub (£) (▶ 97)
- Ⓔ Russell Square, Chancery Lane
- ♿ Limited
- 🎟 Moderate

48 Doughty Street, the birthplace of Oliver Twist, Fagin and a host of other great Dickens characters

ISLE OF DOGS

Map labels: 0 — 500m; EAST INDIA DOCK ROAD; Westferry; All Saints; ASPEN; Poplar; POPLAR; BLACKWALL TUNNEL (Southbound); WAY; PRESTON'S ROAD; Museum in Docklands; West India Quay; Canary Wharf; Billingsgate Fish Market; Heron Quays; West India Docks; South Quay; WEST FERRY ROAD; ISLE OF DOGS; Crossharbour & London Arena; MANCHESTER ROAD; Millwall Docks; CUBITT TOWN; MILLWALL; Mudchute; Thames; Island Gardens; DLR Information Centre; Greenwich Foot Tunnel; Royal Naval College; Greenwich Pier; Cutty Sark; EVELYN STREET; CREEK ROAD; ROMNEY RD; National Maritime Museum; Docklands Light Railway; A

DOCKLANDS ✪✪✪

London's Docklands stretch some 8km (5 miles) east of the Tower of London to the old Royal Docks. Historically, this area was the powerhouse of the Empire, at its height the busiest port in the world. It reached the peak of its activity in 1964 but changes in technology (most notably containerization) signalled its sudden demise. Within a decade most of the quays and great swathes of nearby land were derelict and remained so until the early 1980s when the government began the world's largest urban redevelopment project to date. For an excellent insight into the area's rich history visit the Museum in Docklands, West India Quay (daily 10–6; www.museumindocklands.org).

The centrepiece is Canary Wharf, Britain's tallest building at 243m (797ft). A trip on the Docklands Light Railway (➤ 41) is recommended for its high-level views into this Brave New London World. The latest DLR line, to London City Airport, opened in 2005. Try also the area's historical riverside pubs, which include the Prospect of Whitby, the Mayflower and the Grapes.

Around Docklands

St. Katharine's Dock (► 68) marks the start of London's Docklands. The area goes to sleep at the weekends, so it is best to do this walk on a weekday.

Follow St. Katharine's Way along the river to Wapping High Street.

The old warehouses along here which once held spices and tropical hardwoods have been converted into expensive apartments. At Wapping Pier Head some splendid Georgian houses, once the homes of wealthy wharf owners, can be seen. Beyond Waterside Gardens look at the handsome baroque Church of St. George-in-the-East.

If it is pub opening time (after 11.30am or 12 on Sunday) continue on to the atmospheric old Prospect of Whitby pub (► 97). From here retrace your steps a short way along Wapping Wall, turn right into Garnet Street, cross the main street known as The Highway and turn left then immediately right into Dellow Street, which leads to Shadwell Docklands Light Railway (DLR) station. Board the train for Island Gardens.

You will soon enjoy great views from the high-level track down on to the incredible post-modernist developments that have taken place, and are still in progress, here in the centre of Docklands.

Alight at Island Gardens.

Admire the wonderful view across to Greenwich (► 82–83), and pick up the leaflet 'Amazing Journey' from the DLR office.

Reboard the train and get off at Canary Wharf station.

This is the business and leisure focal point of the new Docklands, with places to eat, drink and shop.

Take a stroll around its redeveloped docks, then either catch the DLR back to Tower Gateway or hop on the underground.

Distance
Walk approximately 3km
(2 miles)

Time
3–4 hours (walk and DLR),
including stops

Start point
St. Katharine's Dock
Tower Hill
⊞ 81D3

End point
Canary Wharf
⊞ 40A2

Lunch
Prospect of Whitby (£) or
various options at Canary
Wharf
✉ 57 Wapping Wall
☎ (020) 7481 1095

Left: *Canary Wharf*
Below: *Docklands
Light Railway*

Dr. Johnson's House

- ✚ 29E3
- ✉ 17 Gough Square
- ☎ (020) 7353 3745; www.drjh.dircon.co.uk
- 🕐 Mon–Sat 11–5.30, (Oct–Apr 11–5)
- 🍴 Ye Olde Cheshire Cheese (£) (► 97)
- 🚇 Chancery Lane, Blackfriars
- ♿ No wheelchair access
- 🖐 Moderate

- ✚ 29F3
- ✉ Guildhall
- ☎ (020) 7606 3030; www.cityoflondon.gov.uk
- 🕐 Great Hall and amphitheatre Mon–Sat 10–4.45; Sun May–Sep 12–4. Closed for ceremonies and events. Art Gallery: Mon–Sat 10–5, Sun 12–4. Clock Museum Mon–Fri 9.30–4.45 ☎ (020) 7332 1868 (ext 1870)
- 🍴 The Place Below (£), St. Mary-le-Bow Church, Cheapside
- 🚇 Bank, St. Paul's, Mansion House
- ♿ Excellent
- 🖐 Great Hall, amphitheatre, Clock Museum free; art gallery inexpensive (free on Fri after 3.30)

FLEET STREET ✪

Fleet Street became the original publishing centre of London in 1500, when England's first press was set up here. From 1702 up to the 1980s it was also the home of England's newspapers until new technology meant they could decamp to cheaper, more efficient offices away from the Street of Ink. Today it is still worth a visit for St. Bride's Church (► 65) and the little alleyways that run north of here. Wine Office Court is home to Ye Olde Cheshire Cheese, while close by is **Dr. Johnson's House**, built *c*1700 and now a museum dedicated to the writer who gave us the first English dictionary.

GUILDHALL ✪

The City of London has been governed from this site for over 800 years and the majestic centrepiece of the Great Hall dates back to 1430. Its huge crypt is older, dating from the mid-13th century and even older are the recently excavated remains of London's only Roman amphitheatre.

The banners and stained-glass coats of arms that decorate the hall belong to the City Livery companies, formed in medieval times to represent and support their professions, and still in existence today. Within the complex is a Clock Museum and the Guildhall Art Gallery featuring 300 years of London art.

Above: Dr. Johnson, a great London wit

Left: The mythical British giant, Magog, at the Guildhall

HAMPSTEAD ✪✪✪

Leafy Hampstead, London's most famous 'village', was developed as a spa in the 18th century and became a fashionable and exclusive retreat favoured by many prominent writers and artists. Spotting name plaques among the many beautiful former homes of luminaries such as Lord Byron, John Keats, H. G. Wells, Robert Louis Stephenson, D. H. Lawrence, John Constable and the like is a favourite visitor pastime. The steep narrow streets around the centre are very well preserved and retain an intimate feel. The most appealing include Flask Walk, Well Walk (where you'll find the original spa fountain), Holly Walk, Hampstead Grove and Church Row. Meanwhile, Hampstead High Street and Heath Street bristle with trendy restaurants, cafés and a good variety of small independent shops that cater to the well-heeled residents.

There are a number of low-key sights in the centre. **Burgh House** acts as a local museum; **Fenton House**, built in 1693, holds ceramics and a renowned collection of historic keyboard instruments; **Keats' House**, where the poet John Keats lived for almost two years, is a delightful spot, where *Ode to a Nightingale* and many other fine poems were written. Just south of here is the **Freud Museum**, where Sigmund Freud lived from 1938 until his death in 1939.

Hampstead's other claim to fame is Hampstead Heath, London's largest and most famous heathland covering some 324ha (800 acres). One of north London's favourite summer walking spots, its ponds are also used for swimming. Parliament Hill is a traditional Sunday venue for kite-flying and offers great views across to central London. Much of the heath consists of undeveloped woodland, the main exception being the landscaped grounds of Kenwood House (➤ 50).

Hampstead
- 80C4
- Hampstead

Tourist Information
- (020) 8348 9908

Burgh House
- New End Square
- (020) 7431 0144
- Wed–Sun 12–5
- Free

Fenton House
- Windmill Hill
- (020) 7435 3471
- Apr–Oct Sat–Sun, public hol Mon 11–5, Wed–Fri 2–5; Mar Sat, Sun 2–5
- Moderate

Keats' House
- Keats Grove
- (020) 7435 2062
- Tue–Sun 1–5
- Moderate

Freud Museum
- 20 Maresfield Gardens
- (020) 7435 2002; www.freud.org.uk
- Wed–Sun 12–5
- Finchley Road
- Moderate

The Holly Bush is a favourite Hampstead hideaway

43

Harrods' Food Halls, a shrine to gourmets and foodies

HARRODS ⭐⭐

Harrods is much more than just a shop, it is an internationally famous institution and even the most reluctant shopper should venture into its cathedral-like portals. The store began trading here in 1849 as a small, family-run grocery shop and by 1911 the present magnificent terracotta building was complete. With a selling area of over 10ha (25 acres) and some 330 departments, it is Britain's biggest department store.

Among the highlights are the lavish and stylish Food Halls. The Meat Hall is gloriously decorated with 1902 tiles, while the focal point fresh-fish display is an extravaganza of the bounty of the sea.

HMS *BELFAST* ⭐

HMS *Belfast* is Europe's last surviving big warship from World War II and occupies a spectacular permanent mooring site on the Thames just upstream from Tower Bridge, opposite Southwark Crown Court. Launched in 1938, she saw action in the Arctic, at the D-Day Normandy landings and in the Korean War from 1950 to 1952

Today her seven cramped labyrinthine decks, which once accommodated a crew of up to 800 men, serve as a museum, giving landlubbers a salty flavour of the rigours of serving at sea. The bridge, galley, operations room, punishment cells, engine and boiler rooms can all be explored. There are also various naval displays. Check out the exhibition Life at Sea.

➕ 28B2
✉ Brompton Road
☎ (020) 7730 1234; www.harrods.com
🕐 Mon–Sat 10–7
🍴 Variety in store (£–£££)
Ⓗ Knightsbridge
♿ Good
❓ No one admitted wearing scruffy clothes, tank tops (men), short shorts or cycling shorts. Backpacks to be left in lockers. Charge for toilets.

➕ 29F3
✉ Morgan's Lane, off Tooley Street
☎ (020) 7940 6300; www.iwm.org.uk
🕐 Daily Mar–Oct 10–6; Nov–Feb 10–5. Closed 24–26 Dec
🍴 Café (£)
Ⓗ London Bridge, Tower Hill. Ferry from Tower Hill pier in summer
♿ None
🎟 Expensive; children free

Did you know ?

The most famous Highgate epitaph belongs to Karl Marx—'Workers of All Lands Unite'—though the most diffident belongs to comedian Max Wall—'... the most I've had is just a talent to amuse'. Carved on the tomb of Tom Sayers, last of the great British bare-fisted boxers, is the huge effigy of his faithful dog, the chief mourner among 10,000 people at the funeral.

The bust of Karl Marx: both an object of pilgrimage and a target of bombers

HIGHGATE ✪✪✪

The charming village of Highgate lies just east of Hampstead Heath and like its famous neighbour, Hampstead (► 43), was a favourite retreat for the upper classes and literary figures, including Samuel Taylor Coleridge (author of *The Rime of the Ancient Mariner*).

Its unlikely, though perennially popular, visitor highlight is Highgate Cemetery. Opened in 1839, the cemetery soon became the fashionable final resting place of politicians, poets, actors and other Victorian personalities. Monuments grew ever larger and more ornate and Highgate Cemetery soon turned into a tourist attraction. The atmospheric West Cemetery is the real draw, piled high with crumbling catacombs, Egyptian columns and obelisks, ivy-clad vaults and grand mausoleums. It looks like the set for a Hammer horror movie and is said to have inspired Bram Stoker (the author of *Dracula*). However, the most famous personalities are buried in the East Cemetery and include Karl Marx, Sir Ralph Richardson, Mary Ann Evans (pen-name George Eliot) and comedian Max Wall.

HOUSES OF PARLIAMENT (► 19, TOP TEN)

HYDE PARK ✪

The largest and most famous of central London's open spaces, Hyde Park covers 138ha (340 acres) and was once the royal hunting ground of Henry VIII and Elizabeth I.

At its northeast corner, at the very end of Oxford Street, is Marble Arch; it was originally erected in front of Buckingham Palace but moved as a result of palace redevelopment. Nearby is Speakers' Corner, London's most famous 'soapbox' where anyone may air their views (within reason).

Flowing through the park is the Serpentine lake, created in 1730, and just west of here is the **Serpentine Gallery**, featuring revolving exhibitions of contemporary art. On the other side of the lake is the unusual and controversial Princess Diana Memorial Fountain, which was opened in 2004 by the Queen.

➕ 80C5
✉ Swain's Lane
☎ (020) 8340 1834
www.highgate-cemetery.org
🕐 East Cemetery Mon–Fri 10–4.30 (3.30 winter), Sat, Sun 11–4.30 (3.30 winter). West Cemetery, admission by tour only; Sat–Sun 11–4 each hour, Mon–Fri tours at 2 (advisable to book). Nov–Mar tours at weekends only 11–3
🍴 Café Mozart, 17 Swain's Lane (£)
🚇 Highgate/Archway
♿ East Cemetery is nearly all freely accessible. The West is partly accessible
💷 Both inexpensive
❓ No children under eight in West Cemetery

➕ 28B2
🕐 Daily at any time
🍴 The Orangery (££), Kensington Gardens
💷 Free
🚇 Marble Arch, Knightsbridge

Serpentine Gallery
☎ (020) 7402 6075; www.serpentinegallery.org
🕐 Daily 10–6 during exhibitions
♿ Excellent 💷 Free
🚇 Lancaster Gate, South Kensington

✚ 29B2
✉ Lambeth Road
☎ (020) 7416 5000; (020)
  7416 5320 (recorded);
  www.iwm.org.uk
🕐 Daily 10–6. Closed 24–26
  Dec
🍴 Café (£), picnic room
  open weekends, school
  hols
🚇 Lambeth North, Elephant
  & Castle, Waterloo
♿ Excellent
🎫 Free
❓ Crimes Against Humanity
  gallery unsuitable for
  under 14s

*The Imperial War
Museum's big naval guns
could once fire an 875kg
(1,925lb) shell a distance
of 30km (19 miles)!*

IMPERIAL WAR MUSEUM ●●●

Dedicated to telling the story of world conflict during the
20th century, the Imperial War Museum has the most
impressive entrance of any London museum. Suspended
from the ceiling of its glass atrium and occupying two
floors around the atrium are World War II fighter planes,
biplanes from the Great War, a V2 rocket, a Polaris missile,
field guns, tanks, submarines, plus over 40 other large
exhibits. Despite this grand martial entrance, however, this
is a thought-provoking museum, which tells the story of
war dispassionately, often from the point of view of the
ordinary soldier or the folks left at home. The emphasis
inevitably is on the two World Wars and each has a large
walk-in section where you can experience the horrors of
the trenches and the claustrophobia of an air-raid shelter,
then the aftermath of a bombing raid. Most harrowing of
all is the permanent exhibition, The Holocaust, and is not
considered suitable for children under 14.

The narrative collection is brilliantly chosen, comprising
many personal and almost everyday objects from the
trenches, the concentration camps, the Far East, the
Eastern Front, the Atlantic Ocean and all the significant
theatres of war. These are combined with memorabilia
such as recruiting posters, dramatic contemporary film
footage and—best of all—spoken first-hand accounts from
ordinary combatants and survivors.

Conflicts since 1945 are also well handled and the
Secret War Exhibition, detailing clandestine operations
from World War I to the present day, is fascinating. The
top floor features the gallery, Crimes Against Humanity.

Around the Inns of Court

This walk should be done on a weekday as not only is the area deserted and devoid of atmosphere at weekends, but several areas within the Inns are closed.

Turn left out of Temple underground station, go up the steps and turn right into Temple Place, which leads (via a car park entrance) to Inner Temple. Turn left up steps to Fountain Court.

The splendid Elizabethan hall and the adjacent gardens are occasionally open.

Continue straight on beneath the archway following the sign to Lamb's Buildings into Middle Temple. Go up the steps to the left of the building ahead to find Temple Church built in 1185 and famous for its effigies of 13th-century Crusader knights. Leave Temple by the alleyway adjacent to Dr. Johnson's Buildings.

At the end is the doorway to Prince Henry's Room, a rare Elizabethan survivor with a fine 17th-century interior.

Cross Fleet Street, turn left and then right alongside the monumental Royal Courts of Justice into Bell Yard. At the end of Bell Yard turn left and, by Legastat printers, turn right into New Square, the heart of Lincoln's Inn.

Lincoln's Inn's splendid hall (to the left) isn't open but you can visit the chapel (to the right, ◷ 12–2.30), built in 1620.

Continue through the Inn and exit right at the corner of Stone Buildings. Cross Chancery Lane, turn right, then go left into Southampton Buildings, which leads to Staple Inn.

This is a former Inn of Chancery (a prep school for the Inns of Court); note its Elizabethan façade on High Holborn.

Cross High Holborn, turn left, then, by the Cittie of York pub, go right into Gray's Inn. Duck beneath the arch to the left of the hall (closed) to Gray's Inn Gardens. Return to High Holborn for Chancery Lane tube.

Distance
Approximately 4km (2.5 miles)

Time
2–3 hours depending on visits

Start point
◉ Temple (closed Sun)
✚ 29D3

End point
◉ Chancery Lane (closed Sun)
✚ 29D4

Lunch
Cittie of York, Holborn (£)

Middle Temple Hall
☎ (020) 7936 2710
◷ Mon–Fri 10–12, 3–4

Middle Temple Gardens
◷ May–Jul, Sep
Mon–Fri 12–3

Prince Henry's Room
✉ 17 Fleet Street
☎ (020) 7936 4004
◷ Mon–Sat 11–2

♿ All free

The Temple Church

🔒 29D3
🟢 Green Park, Piccadilly Circus
♿ None
✋ Free

INNS OF COURT ✪✪✪

The Inns of Court, the training grounds for the country's barristers, date from medieval times. Today there are just four surviving: Inner Temple, Middle Temple, Lincoln's Inn and Gray's. Each resembles a small college campus, with a library, chapel, hall and barristers' chambers. Their grounds, usually open to the public from Monday to Friday, are central London's most charming and peaceful oases, and their narrow alleyways and small courtyards, many still gaslit, are very atmospheric in the early evening (► 47).

🔒 28C3
🟢 Green Park, Piccadilly Circus

JERMYN STREET ✪✪

Jermyn (pronounced German) Street is a slice of traditional 'Gentleman's London', famous for its exclusive and elegant shops. Cigar smokers should look in at Davidoff, while pipe smokers will enjoy Dunhill. Don't miss Floris (at No. 89), Paxton & Whitfield (No. 93) and Bates the Hatter (No. 21a) featuring Binks the cat, stuffed in 1926, in a black top hat.

🔒 29D2
✉ Old Palace Yard, Abingdon Street
☎ (020) 7222 2219; www.english-heritage.org.uk
🕐 Daily Apr–Oct 19–5; Nov–Mar 10–4
🍽 The Cinnamon Club (£££), Great Smith Street
　　☎ (020) 7222 2555
🟢 Westminster, St. James's Park
♿ None
✋ Cheap

JEWEL TOWER ✪

This venerable, solitary tower is one of the few remaining parts of the old Palace of Westminster (► 19). Built in 1366, it was used to house the personal valuables of Edward III and was known as the Royal Wardrobe. Today it makes an excellent introduction to the Houses of Parliament with an exhibition about their history and procedural practices. You can also take a 'tour' of Parliament on a multimedia touch-screen machine.

The Jewel Tower once held the king's jewels, furs, clothes and gold vessels

KENSINGTON PALACE AND KENSINGTON GARDENS

⭐⭐⭐

William III was the first monarch to set up home in Kensington Palace, in 1689, and it was here in 1819 that the future Queen Victoria was born. Royal patronage continues with several members of the present royal family having palace apartments. In September 1997 it was a focus of the country's grief as the last home of the late Princess Diana, when thousands of floral tributes were piled up in front of the palace gates. There is no memorial within the palace to Diana but a memorial playground is close by in Kensington Gardens.

The fabric of the present palace, which actually resembles a country house in both style and size, dates largely from the early 18th century. The parts that are open to the visitor divide broadly into two areas: the State Apartments and the Royal Ceremonial Dress Collection. The Apartments are striking for their magnificent ceiling paintings by William Kent and some impressive and curious *trompe-l'œil* effects. The Royal Ceremonial Dress Collection features a superb collection of court finery. Surrounding the palace are pretty sunken gardens and a red-brick orangery, now a restaurant.

Outside the palace gates is Kensington Gardens, which runs east into Hyde Park. This pretty lawned expanse boasts two famous statues. To the north is Peter Pan, and to the south, near the Royal Albert Hall, is the amazingly intricate Albert Memorial 53m (174ft) high which is dedicated to Prince Albert, Queen Victoria's much-loved consort.

✚ 80C3
✉ Kensington Gardens
☎ (020) 7937 9561; www.hrp.org.uk
🕐 Daily Mar–Oct 10–5 (last admission); Nov–Feb 10–4 (last admission)
🍴 The Orangery (££)
Ⓜ High Street Kensington, Queensway
♿ Limited
💷 Very expensive
❓ Guided tours available

The gates of Kensington Palace became a sad place of pilgrimage after the death of Princess Diana in 1997

KENWOOD HOUSE ⭐⭐

+ 80C5
✉ Hampstead Lane
☎ (020) 8348 1286; www.
english-heritage.org.uk
🕐 Daily 10–5 (10.30–5 Wed,
Fri). Closes 4 Nov–Mar.
Closed 24, 25 Dec, 1 Jan
🍴 Restaurant, café (£–££)
🚇 Hampstead, then bus 210
♿ Good
🎟 Free (charge: exhibitions)

*Part of Adam's beautiful
library in Kenwood House*

If you would like to see a real country house without leaving central London then Kenwood, on the north of Hampstead Heath (► 43), fits the bill perfectly. It was remodelled in 1764 by Robert Adam, whose signature pale blue, neo-classical design (made famous by Wedgwood pottery) is immediately apparent on entry to the house. The paintings at Kenwood are known as the Iveagh Bequest and form one of the most important collections bequeathed to the nation. They are mostly 17th- and 18th-century works from the English, Dutch and French schools, though recent additions include much earlier paintings by Botticelli and Hans Memling. The most

famous is a Rembrandt self-portrait, acknowledged as one of his very best. Also notable are works by Frans Hals and Vermeer. The architectural *tour de force* of the house is the library, with its elaborately decorated tunnel-vaulted ceiling and Corinthian columns. It is considered one of Adam's finest interiors.

The beautiful gardens at Kenwood are the most cultivated part of Hampstead Heath, with a lawned amphitheatre sloping down to a lake. During the summer this becomes London's finest outdoor classical music venue—American visitors note, Handel's *Fireworks Music* is played every 4 July with accompanying pyrotechnics!

LEIGHTON HOUSE ⭐⭐

+ 80C3
✉ 12 Holland Park Road
☎ (020) 7602 3316;
www.rbkc.gov.uk
🕐 Wed–Mon 11–5:30
🍴 Several on High Street
Kensington (£–££)
🚇 High Street Kensington
♿ None
🎟 Moderate

The distinguished Victorian artist Frederic Lord Leighton (1830–96) created this beautiful romantic house between 1864 and 1866 and lived here until his death in 1896. The centrepiece is the Arab Hall, a glorious mini-Alhambra featuring a dome from Damascus, window screens from Cairo and Leighton's highly valued, rare collection of 15th- and 16th-century Islamic tiles from Cairo, Damascus and Rhodes. The other rooms are much more restrained but contain some fine works by Lord Leighton and his famous Pre-Raphaelite associates.

Left: *Lloyd's of London's space-age building.*
Below: *Lloyd's doormen in 17th-century attire*

LLOYD'S BUILDING ⊗⊗

Designed by Richard Rogers, of Georges Pompidou Centre (Paris) fame, and sharing the same characteristic of wearing its guts on its sleeve, this stunning glass and steel tower ('a post-modern oil refinery' said one critic) was the most controversial building in England when finished in 1986. It is closed to the public but remains one of London's most potent architectural statements.

⊞ 29F3
✉ Leadenhall Street
🚫 Closed to public
🍴 Leadenhall Wine Bar (£), Leadenhall Market
🚇 Aldgate

LONDON AQUARIUM ⊗⊗

This is the capital's first real aquarium and one of the new generation of maximum-visibility, large-tank, natural-atmosphere aquaria that are currently enjoying great popularity. Giant tanks, 8m (26ft) high, feature Atlantic and Pacific displays. The latter is home to sand tiger and brown sharks, and large rays that glide silently between giant, sunken, replica Easter Island statues. The Reef and Living Coral exhibit and the Indian Ocean tank is where you can watch the sharks and piranhas feed, listen to rainforest talks, while the highlight for many children is the chance to stroke a ray in the touch pool.

⊞ 29D2
✉ County Hall, Riverside Building, Westminster Bridge Road
☎ (020) 7967 8000; londonaquarium.co.uk
🕐 Daily 10–6
🍴 Options on premises and in County Hall
🚇 Waterloo, Westminster
♿ Excellent 🏷 Expensive

In the Know

If you only have a short time to visit London, or would like to get a real flavour of the city, here are some ideas:

10
Ways To Be a Local

Read *Time Out* for What's On and the *London Evening Standard*.
Put on some comfortable shoes and walk It's often the best, and sometimes the quickest, way to get around.
Shop at one of the many street markets.

Settle down to watch a game of cricket on Kew Green.
Take a historic walking tour.
Eat in one of London's few surviving pie 'n' mash shops (➤ 96).
Ride the top deck of any regular London bus.
Buy a sandwich and eat it in one of London's parks, or if you're in the city, in a churchyard.
Go to Speaker's Corner on a Sunday morning.
See the Changing of the Guard at Horse Guards, Whitehall (➤ 77).

10
Good Places to Have Lunch

The Orangery (££–£££)
✉ Kensington Palace Gardens. Part-designed by Wren. Go for tea. No telephone bookings.
Jason's (£££)
✉ Opposite 60 Blomfield Road, Maida Vale.
☎ (020) 7286 6752. Modern European in a beautiful canalside setting.
The Ritz Hotel (£££)
✉ 150 Piccadilly
☎ (020) 7493 8181. Palatial luxury at a set price.
The Belvedere (£££)
✉ Holland Park ☎ (020) 7602 1238. Great views and a beautiful setting.
Café-in-the-Crypt (£)
✉ St. Martin-in-the-Fields, Duncannon Street,
☎ (020) 7839 4342. This

oasis of calm will provide a welcome break from the frenzy of Trafalgar Square.
World Food Café (£)
✉ Neal's Yard, Covent Garden ☎ (020) 7379 0298. One of a choice of wholefood eateries set in a charming courtyard.
Odette's (£££)
✉ 130 Regent's Park Road ☎ (020) 7586 5486. Excellent food served in the garden.
Imperial China (£)
✉ White Bear Yard, 25a Lisle Street ☎ (020) 7734 3388. For some of Chinatown's best *dim sum*.
Prêt à Manger (£)
For lunch on the move; good-quality fresh hand-made snacks and sandwiches. Branches all over central London.
A London Park (£–£££)
Regent's Park, Greenwich Park, Hampstead Heath. Take a picnic.

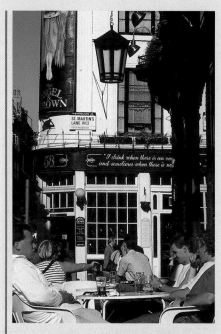

A typical London pub

The Lamb
✉ 94 Lamb's Conduit Street. Dickens reputedly enjoyed a drink here. Unspoilt Victorian gem with original sepia photographs of music hall stars. Good food and beer.

Lamb Tavern
✉ 10–12 Leadenhall Market. Superb Grade II listed tavern in the famous markert. Original tiling throughout. Said to have the best roast beef sandwiches in town.

Salisbury
✉ 90 St. Martin's Lane. Bustling, beautifully preserved Victorian pub at the heart of Theatreland.

Spaniards
✉ Spaniard's Road, Hampstead Heath. Bags of history and a lovely garden.

10

Best London Vantage Points

St. Paul's Cathedral (➤ 22)
Parliament Hill (➤ 43)
British Airways London Eye (➤ 33)
Oxo Tower (➤ 63)
Hilton Hotel, Hyde Park (➤ 97 side panel)
Tower Bridge (➤ 74)
The Monument (➤ 56)
Tower 42 Formerly known as the NatWest Tower this colossus, 183m (600ft) high, features restaurant Rhodes Twentyfour on the 24th floor and Vertigo bar on the 42nd.
Greenwich Park, Old Royal Observatory (➤ 83)
Waterloo Bridge (➤ 9)

Left: *Eating alfresco*
Far left: *Petticoat Lane street market*

10

Good Pubs

Cittie of York
✉ 22 High Holborn. A pub has stood on this site since 1430. Rebuilt in its present form in 1685 as Gray's Inn Coffee House. Impressive vaulted rear bar.

Cross Keys
✉ 1 Lawrence Street. A fine Chelsea pub dating from 1765. Stylish with an open-plan conservatory.

Fox & Anchor
✉ 115 Charterhouse Street. Atmospheric Smithfield market pub with unique opening hours to suit the workers (7am–9pm Monday to Friday).

Grenadier
✉ Old Barrack Yard, Wilton Row. Fine 18th-century Knightsbridge mews pub. Largely undiscovered by tourists.

5

Top Activities

Take to the water in Docklands for sailing, rowing etc at Docklands Watersports Centre (☎ (020) 7537 2626).

Go horseback riding in Hyde Park (➤ 115).

Row on the Thames at Richmond (☎ (020) 8948 8270).

Indulge yourself at The Sanctuary, Covent Garden (ladies only)—a wonderful, if expensive, health club (☎ 0870 770 3350).

Ice skate in the heart of the City at Broadgate Ice Rink from late October to early April (☎ (020) 7505 4068).

🕂 29F2

✉ Tooley Street

☎ (020) 7403 0606
(recorded information);
(020) 7403 7221 (general
enquiries);
www.thedungeons.com

🕐 Daily: 10–6 (last
admission 5). Closed
25 Dec

🍴 Butler's Wharf Chop
House, 36E Shad Thames
(£££) (➤ 92)

🚇 London Bridge

♿ Excellent

💷 Very expensive

Prepare to be terrified by the sight and sounds of the London Dungeon

LONDON DUNGEON ●●

'Abandon hope all who enter here' is the message of the London Dungeon, the world's first and foremost museum of medieval (and other) horrors. It was begun in 1975 by a London housewife whose children were disappointed by the lack of blood and gore on display at the Tower of London. Certainly no one leaves the Dungeon with such complaints! The dark tunnels beneath London Bridge now include many more blood-curdling special effects, with a 'dark ride' (in every sense) and costumed actors to enhance the scream factor. Ghouls and the curious, including most of London's overseas teenagers, make this one of the capital's most visited attractions, but this is definitely not a place for young children or the faint of heart.

🕂 28B4

✉ Marylebone Road

☎ (0870) 400 3000;
www.madame-
tussauds.com

🕐 Mon–Fri shows from
12.30; Sat, Sun from
10.30. (➤ 56 for further
details for Madame
Tussauds)

LONDON PLANETARIUM (AUDITORIUM) ●

This is actually part of Madame Tussaud's (➤ 56), and has been renamed Auditorium. This planetarium is devoted to the exploration of space. The shows are put on every 30 minutes and there are entertaining and educational interactive exhibition areas that visitors can explore and enjoy while they are waiting. The show itself (which is changed periodically) is a mixture of traditional planetarium star-gazing and modern 3-D space adventures using projection and simulator techniques.

🕂 29D3

✉ Covent Garden

🕐 Closed until early 2007
for major expansion and
redevelopment

LONDON'S TRANSPORT MUSEUM ●●

At first glance a museum of London Transport may not look terribly interesting, but if you want to wallow in a little London nostalgia or if you have children in tow you can easily spend an enjoyable couple of hours here. The mainstay of the collection is its handsome historical hardware—evocative old double-deckers, the earliest horse-drawn London buses, a steam-driven train that ran underground (and managed to consume its own smoke) and so on. However, it is also very much a hands-on museum, with lots of activities for children and adults. You can ring bells, clamber on vehicles and if you think you could have driven the bus or underground train as well as the driver who brought you here, then take the simulator controls and find out. Closed until early 2007.

LONDON ZOO ⭐⭐

Opened in 1828, this was the world's first serious zoo. It soon achieved worldwide fame and reached its peak in the 1950s, when visitor numbers topped over 3 million per year. In recent times, however, as a result of current opinion regarding captive animals and a new generation of open, cage-free zoos, attendances fell so dramatically that it too was put on the endangered list. Now, thankfully, its future is secure and even though too many of its cages and enclosures are still small and old-fashioned, it still makes an enjoyable family day out for most visitors.

The zoo is not overly large but it's best to plan your day around the timetable of activities, such as feeding times, talks, shows and the entertaining Animals in Action presentations. Other highlights include the Mappin Terrace sloth bears, the penguin pool and the Snowdon Aviary. The elephants and rhinos have been moved to Whipsnade Zoo to allow them more space.

- 🟦 80C4
- ✉ Regent's Park
- ☎ (020) 7722 3333; www.londonzoo.co.uk
- 🕑 Daily Mar–Oct 10–5.30; Nov–Feb 10–4. Last admission 1 hour before closing. Closed 25 Dec
- 🍴 Café-restaurant (£)
- Ⓜ Camden Town
- ♿ Good
- 🖐 Very expensive

Above: *Penguins play on the slides above the pool at London Zoo*

Did you know ?

That it was London Zoo's very first elephant, named Jumbo (acquired in 1867), who gave his name to any object of giant size (such as the jumbo jet). The elephants were such a novelty that they became the talk of London and so frantic was the 'elephant-mania' that Jumbo's mate, Alice, lost some 30cm (12in) of her trunk to a ruthless souvenir hunter!

28B4

✉ Marylebone Road

☎ (0870) 400 3000;
www.madame-
tussauds.com

🕐 Mon–Fri 9.30–5.30,
Sat, Sun 9–6. Closed
25 Dec

🍴 Café (£)

🚇 Baker Street

♿ Spirit of London ride
not accessible to
wheelchairs

💷 Very expensive

❓ To avoid waiting in line
book in advance by
credit card

MADAME TUSSAUD'S ✪✪✪

The grand old dame of London tourism, Madame T's has for several years been the capital's top entrance-paid attraction, as infamous for its queues (which you can now

avoid) as for the excellence of its lifelike figures. Madame Tussaud began her career making death masks of guillotine victims, moved to England in 1802 and set up in London in 1835. You can still see objects of the French Revolution, including the waxworks' oldest figure— Madame Dubarry (Louis XV's mistress), made in 1765. She is cast as The Sleeping Beauty, with an ingenious breathing mechanism to keep her slumbering eternally. You can't touch her, but you can give Brad Pitt a squeeze or make J-Lo blush and the interactive theme continues allowing you to become a star on Madame T's television. There's a special Spiderman feature too.

The World Stage brings together politicians and royalty, while The Chamber of Horrors is more horrible than ever with live actors to incite even more shock factor (unsuitble for the under 12s). Far better to whisk younger children off on the enjoyable Disney-like Spirit of London ride, replete with anima-tronic figures and special effects.

For details of the Audiorium, formerly known as The London Planetarium, ➤ 54.

Above: *Madame T's is a capital institution*

Right: *The Monument was once a favourite London suicide spot*

 29F3

✉ Monument Street

☎ (020) 7626 2717

🕐 Daily 10–6

🍴 Leadenhall Wine Bar (£),
Leadenhall Market

🚇 Monument

♿ None

💷 Moderate

MONUMENT ✪

The Monument is the world's highest free-standing column; it measures 62m (203ft), which is exactly the distance due east to the site of the bakery in Pudding Lane where the Great Fire of London began in 1666. It was commissioned by King Charles II 'to preserve the memory of this dreadful Visitation' and designed jointly by Christopher Wren and Robert Hooke. You can climb the inside of the column via a 311-step spiral staircase and enjoy views of the City.

MUSEUM OF CHILDHOOD, BETHNAL GREEN ✪✪

The Museum of Childhood actually started life in 1856 in South Kensington as a temporary wing of the Victoria and Albert Museum. Its elaborate, typically Victorian ironwork structure was then moved wholesale to Bethnal Green and, aside from comfy carpets, new glass cases and a 1990s café, little has changed since. Today it is still part of the V&A and is a shrine to childhood and all the accoutrements that go with it; from birthing stools to children's wartime gas masks, from Javanese shadow puppets and Steiff teddy bears to Sonic the Hedgehog and Teletubbies. Parents should note that the museum is as much for adults as for children, documenting social trends and changes through the medium of play. Many toys date back centuries and several are exquisite hand-made pieces. The museum is particularly renowned for its collection of doll's houses, most of which were never intended as playthings. Its doll collection is also comprehensive and includes some outstanding Japanese ceremonial dolls. Parents and grandparents get dewy eyed reminiscing about long-lost, long-forgotten toys while their offspring amuse themselves at various play areas around the museum. There are regular children's activities and events workshops, theatre productions and a soft-play area is open each Sunday.

🔲 81E4
✉ Cambridge Heath Road
☎ (020) 8980 2415 (24-hour information);
www.vam.ac.uk
🕐 Sat–Thu 10–5.50
🍴 Café (sandwiches only)
(£)
🚇 Bethnal Green
♿ Excellent
💷 Free
❓ Lovely park next door for picnics

The Museum of Childhood was moved lock, stock and barrel to Bethnal Green in the East End from its original home in South Kensington

29E3

London Wall

(020) 7600 3699.
Information line (020)
7600 0807;
www.museumoflondon.
org.uk

Mon–Sat 10–5.50, Sun
12–5.50. Last admission
5.30. Closed 24–26 Dec,
1 Jan

Good café-restaurant (£)

Barbican, St. Paul's,
Moorgate

Excellent

Free

Family events, including
costumed actors, most
Suns and during school
hols

MUSEUM OF LONDON

Reputed to be the most comprehensive city museum in the world, the multi-award-winning Museum of London tells you everything you ever wanted to know about the history of the capital. The displays are engaging and the captions punchy and entertaining. There's a lot to explore, and it might prove difficult to see it all during one visit.

Displays are chronological, starting with the new prehistory gallery that follows the story of Londoners before Roman settlement, progressing to Roman London. The latter is a highlight, with reconstructed rooms and superb sculptures from the Temple of Mithras discovered close by. Another new exhibition, the Medieval gallery shows objects from recent excavations, never displayed before, shedding light on the Dark Ages of the 15th century and going through more enlightened times up to 1558. Highlights include an audio-visual on the Black Death, a reconstruction of an Anglo-Saxon home and objects from 13th-century Jewish houses in the City of London. In the Stuart section you will find Oliver Cromwell's death mask, the Cheapside (jewellery) Hoard, plague exhibits and the Great Fire Experience, accompanied by a reading from the diary of Samuel Pepys.

Further galleries, from late Stuart times to the present, feature many fascinating large-scale exhibits. Most handsome of all is the opulent Lord Mayor's State Coach, made in 1757. The World City galleries cover the period from the French Revolution to the outbreak of World War I, and in the Victorian Walk section are some fascinating reconstructions of London shop fronts.

The largest and best-preserved Roman mosaic in London, which can be seen at the Museum of London

This superb mid-18th century Grenadier Officer's cap is one of many uniforms on display at the National Army Museum

NATIONAL ARMY MUSEUM ⭐

The first professional British Army was formed in 1485 and this museum, recently refurbished and upgraded, covers its history in the five centuries to date. Audio-visual presentations, dioramas and lifelike soldier mannequins bring to life the lot of the ordinary soldier in a manner that concentrates more on the daily hardships than on the glory of war.

Start in the basement with Redcoats, which moves from Agincourt to the American War of Independence. As well as a fine display of swords you can try on a civil war helmet and feel the weight of a cannon shot.

The Road to Waterloo follows the story of the soldiers in Wellington's army and includes a huge, scale model of the battlefield (at the critical moment of 7.15pm on 18 June 1815) and the skeleton of Napoleon's beloved war horse, Marengo. Move on briskly through the Victorian Soldier exhibitions noting Florence Nightingale's lamp, quite unlike the lantern of popular imagination. The Brixmis exhibition on information gathered during the Cold War is also surprisingly interesting.

Displays on the two World Wars and the modern British Army (1965 to date) bring the story up to date, though if you are particularly interested in this period you would be better off paying a visit to the Imperial War Museum (▶ 46).

✚ 28B1
✉ Royal Hospital Road, Chelsea
☎ (020) 7730 0717; www.national-army-museum.ac.uk
🕐 Daily 10–5.30. Closed 24–26 Dec, 1 Jan, Good Fri, May Day public hol
🍴 Café (£)
🚇 Sloane Square, then 10 minutes' walk along King's Road into Smith Street
♿ Excellent
🎟 Free
❓ A lively range of activities is often staged—see the *What's On* leaflets

Food & Drink

Long the butt of culinary jokes, the capital's restaurants and British cooking have improved so much in recent years that London is now regarded as among the best places in the world for eating out. The only drawback is that this can be expensive, but fixed-price meals, particularly at lunchtime, can make your pound go very much further.

What To Eat

The world is your oyster, with representatives from virtually every culinary school on the planet. The most acclaimed generally fall under the banner of Modern European cuisine. When in Britain, however, it would be a shame not to eat British food, from traditional hearty English dishes to the more sophisticated, foreign-influenced, eclectic Modern British cuisine. Long assimilated into mainstream British culture, Indian food should also be on your personal menu. And of course, at the end of the night look for the nearest fish and chip shop!

Where To Eat

At the cutting edge of the market the current vogue is for restaurants to boast huge dining rooms, with some likened to ocean liners. Restaurant fashion seems almost as important as the food itself and many of London's leading eating houses are owned by renowned design guru Sir Terence Conran.

Fashion pervades all the way down the price scale, with yesterday's humble cafés making way for today's trendy *cafès*. In line with this trend, museum catering has improved enormously in the last few years, too.

If you're on a tight budget, are not concerned with frills, but want to avoid fast-food insipidity, you'll still be able to find one of London's myriad cheap and cheerful old-fashioned Italian family-run cafés.

Above: *Grab lunch in Ye Olde Cheshire Cheese*
Below: *Afternoon tea*

When, Where and What To Drink

London is no longer straitjacketed by antiquated licensing laws and, consequently, you can now drink alcohol at most times of the day or night. As with restaurants, there are any number of different styles of bar, many of the designer variety. These can be so expensive and so busy admiring their own reflection that it's a wonder they get any custom. London has many fine traditional English pubs serving traditional English beer. At its best, it is hand-drawn from oak casks and is darker and warmer than lager beers.

British Food

There are places still serving the type of food Charles Dickens would recognize—hot savoury pies, roast meats and game, and to follow steamed sweet puddings and pies—though they don't usually come cheap. The traditional British Sunday lunch (roast beef and Yorkshire pudding) is a must; try one of our recommended British restaurants or any good large hotel.

Wherever you are staying you will probably get the chance to start the day the traditional British way, with a cooked breakfast of eggs, bacon and/or sausages, mushrooms, tomatoes and/or baked beans and toast. Afternoon tea is the other great English institution, comprising small thinly sliced sandwiches, scones and/or cake. At many of London's famous hotels, such as the Ritz, afternoon tea is an important daily ritual.

Look for hand-pumped beer if you want a quality pint

A typical London pub along Whitehall

Below: *The world's most comprehensive portrait collection at the National Portrait Gallery*

✚ 29D3

✉ St Martin's Place, Orange Street

☎ (020) 7306 0055; www.npg.org.uk

🕐 Daily 10–6 (Thu, Fri until 9). Closed 24–26 Dec, 1 Jan, Good Fri, May Day public hol

🍴 Rooftop restaurant (££), café (£)

Ⓜ Leicester Square, Charing Cross

♿ Excellent (use Orange Street entrance)

🎟 Free (except special exhibitions)

❓ Audio guides to over 350 portraits; frequent lectures and tours

---

Did you know ?

The raffish picture of William Shakespeare, the Chandos Portrait (painted c1610), is the sole known contemporary portrait of the Bard of Avon and is therefore claimed to be his only true likeness. It was the first picture to enter the gallery. On a similar note, there are also few original portraits of Christopher Wren in existence and the National Portrait Gallery's is one of the best.

NATIONAL PORTRAIT GALLERY ❂❂❂

If you've ever wanted to put a face to a famous name from British history then this is the place to do it. Founded in 1856 as the 'Gallery of the Portraits of the most eminent persons in British History', the gallery's earliest contemporary portrait is that of Henry VII, from 1505. If you want to see the exhibits in chronological order go up to the top floor and work your way down. The collection is too large to be displayed at one time so changes periodically. The pictures least likely to change are the oldest, many of which are of great historical value. Those most likely to be rotated are the portraits of late 20th-century figures; the display of new additions tends to be dictated by current public interest.

Most visitors' favourites are the very earliest (top floor), the most recent, the Victorian and the early 20th century galleries. Predictably, there are many images of royalty, and at opposite ends of the gallery is a wonderful contrast of styles featuring the likenesses of Elizabeth I and, some 400 years later, the present British queen, Elizabeth II. The Coronation Portrait of Elizabeth I is an acclaimed masterpiece, while much more controversial is the colour screenprint, in signature fashion by Andy Warhol, of the current monarch. This also underlines the point that the gallery holds more than just conventional paintings; sculptures, photography, sketches, silhouettes, caricatures and other methods of portraiture are all featured. Among contemporary portraits you'll find soccer star David Beckham, musician Sir Paul McCartney and actress, Catherine Zeta-Jones.

NATURAL HISTORY MUSEUM
(► 21, TOP TEN)

OXO TOWER

Built in 1930 for the Oxo company, this splendid art deco tower has long been a Thames landmark, but in recent times had fallen into such disrepair that demolition was a likelihood. Now lovingly restored, its huge illuminated red O X O trademark letters make it one of the most striking sights on the London night skyline. The tower is now home to exhibition spaces, eating places (open daily), award-winning craft and designer shops and studios (closed Monday). Another good reason for visiting it is to enjoy the panoramic views from the free 8th-floor public viewing gallery.

29E3
Riverside Walk
(020) 7401 2255;
www.oxotower.co.uk
Viewing gallery 11–10
Various (£–£££)
Blackfriars, Waterloo
Accessible by lift
Free

PICCADILLY CIRCUS

London's most famous circus (a site where several streets meet) is almost permanently clogged with traffic and young tourists who use the steps around the Statue of Eros as a convenient rest stop or meeting point. The statue actually represents the Angel of Christian Charity not the Greek God of love. Piccadilly Circus is a frenetic, unattractive place, best seen at night when the illuminated hoardings come to life. Just off here is the rather tacky Trocadero, claimed to be Europe's largest indoor entertainment complex (► 111).

28C3
Piccadilly Circus

Sooner or later everyone walks through Piccadilly Circus

✚ 28B4

🍽 Odette's (££–£££)

◉ South of park: Regent's Park, Baker Street. North of park: Camden Town

♿ Excellent

🎟 Free

Right: *Pigeon fancier in Regent's Park*
Below: *Sir Joshua Reynolds, founder of the Royal Academy in 1768*

✚ 28C3

✉ Burlington House, Piccadilly

☎ (020) 7300 8000. Advance tickets 0870 848 8484; www.royal academy.org.uk

◉ Daily during exhibition 10–6 (Fri, Sat until 10). Fine Rooms Tue–Fri 1–4.30; Sat, Sun 10–6. Closed 25 Dec

🍽 Café (£), self-service restaurant (££)

◉ Green Park, Piccadilly Circus

♿ Excellent

🎟 Expensive

REGENT'S PARK ⓿⓿⓿

Like many of London's parks, this land was appropriated by Henry VIII as a royal hunting ground and was not known as Regent's Park until 1820, when the Prince Regent (the future George IV) decided to develop it as a grand new garden city. His architect, John Nash, was also responsible for much of the magnificent building of Bath (➤ 88). The beautiful white sweeps of stuccoed buildings that make up the park's terraces and crescents represent only a small part of the original plans, but they remain the most elegant example of town planning in the capital.

The gardens, delightful in summer, are famous for the Zoo, Queen Mary's Rose Garden and the Regent's Park Open-air Theatre (➤ 112). You can also go boating on the lake.

ROYAL ACADEMY (OF ARTS) ⓿⓿⓿

The RA is the country's oldest fine arts society and regularly stages world-class art exhibitions, most famously the annual Summer Exhibition (in June). The elegant home of the RA, Burlington House, features some fine 18th-century ceiling paintings and has recently opened its Fine Rooms to provide a permanent display space. This includes major works by leading British artists from Reynolds to Hockney, plus Britain's sole Michelangelo sculpture.

ST. BARTHOLOMEW-THE-GREAT ⊙⊙

Founded in 1123 by Rahere, the court jester to Henry I, this is London's oldest church. The entrance is an unusual half-timbered Tudor gatehouse, and the atmospheric interior is reminiscent of a small cathedral. It has the best Norman chancel in London (rivalled only by the Chapel of St John in the Tower of London ➤ 24) with Norman piers supporting an upper gallery. There are also some very fine tomb monuments, including that of Rahere.

🚩 29C4
✉ West Smithfield
☎ (020) 7606 5171; www.greatstbarts.com
🕐 Tue–Fri 8.30–5 (4 in winter), Sat 10.30–1.30, Sun 8.30–1, 2.30–8
🍴 Fox and Anchor (£)
🚇 Barbican
♿ Access to most parts
🎫 Free

Did you know ?

The landmark spire of St Bride's, a 'madrigal in stone' and the tallest of any Wren church at 69m (226ft), is said to be the model for the traditional tiered wedding cake. These were first made around 200 years ago by Mr Rich, a Fleet Street pastry-cook who became famous for his spire-inspired confections.

Above: *The tomb of Rahere in St. Bart's. He was buried in 1143, but the monument dates from the 16th century*
Left: *Wren's masterpiece tower at St. Bride's*

ST. BRIDE'S ⊙

The Church of St. Bride occupies one of the capital's oldest religious sites; during the 6th century St. Bridget's Church marked the very first Irish settlement in London. The present church, completed in 1675, is a masterpiece by Christopher Wren though its interior is modern, having been gutted by a bomb in 1940. The crypt holds an interesting small museum tracing the history of the church and its long connection with the Fleet Street newspaper trade.

🚩 29E3
✉ Fleet Street
☎ (020) 7427 0133; www.stbrides.com
🕐 Mon–Fri 8–5, Sat phone in advance, Sun, open for services only at 11, 6.30
🍴 Ye Olde Cheshire Cheese (£)
🚇 Blackfriars
♿ Access to church via Salisbury Court side entrance; crypt inaccessible
🎫 Free
❓ Lunchtime concerts (most of year, not Lent and Dec) Tue, Wed, Fri 1.15, choral services Sun 11, 6.30

ST. JAMES'S PALACE ✪

After the Palace of Whitehall was destroyed in 1698, the court moved to St. James's Palace, which remained the official royal London residence until 1837, when Queen Victoria decamped to Buckingham Palace. Sadly, little remains of the palace's Tudor structure except for the splendid main gatehouse in Pall Mall. The Chapel Royal also retains its original exterior. Adjacent to the palace is **Clarence House**, formerly home to the late Queen Mother, but now occupied by the Prince of Wales. Like Buckingham Palace, it is now open to the public for a short period during the summer.

✚ 28C2
✉ Chapel Royal, St. James's Palace
⏰ Open for services only Sun 8.30, 11.15 (see notice board on door to confirm or visit www.royal.gov.uk)
🍴 Quaglino's (£££) (➤ 95)
Ⓖ Green Park
♿ Chapel Royal accessible to wheelchairs
▨ Free
❓ The St. James's Palace detachment of the Queen's Guard marches to Buckingham Palace at 11.15 and returns to St. James's Palace at 12.05. The Guard is changed only on days when there is a guard change at Buckingham Palace

Clarence House
⏰ Aug to mid-Oct daily 9.30–6 by guided tour only
☎ (020) 7766 7303; www.royal.gov.uk
▨ Moderate

Guardsmen at St. James's Palace preparing to march off to change the guard at Buckingham Palace

ST JAMES'S PARK ✪✪

The oldest and the prettiest of central London's royal parks, St. James's was established by Henry VIII in the 1530s. Charles II was the last monarch to reshape it and was often to be seen walking in the park with one of his many mistresses, or swimming in its lake. Don't miss the magical views from the bridge in the centre of the lake, west to Buckingham Palace and east to the domes and towers of Whitehall.

✚ 28C2
Ⓖ St James's Park
▨ Free

ST. JAMES'S PICCADILLY ⭐

This 'little piece of heaven in Piccadilly' was built between 1676 and 1684 by Christopher Wren, though it was badly damaged in World War II and has largely been rebuilt. The main artistic interest of the church is the work of Grinling Gibbons, the greatest woodcarver in 17th-century England. However, the church's popularity, particularly with local Londoners, lies in the numerous cultural activities it promotes, including an arts and crafts market, an antiques market and regular top-class concerts and recitals.

ST JAMES'S STREET ⭐⭐

St James's is 'Gentlemen's London' and here you will find four of its most distinguished clubs: White's (No. 37–8), where Prince Charles held his stag party in 1981; Boodle's (No. 28), haunt of London's chief 19th-century dandy, Beau Brummell; Brooks's (No. 60), renowned for its gambling; and the Carlton (No. 69), bastion of the Conservative party whose male-only rules were bent for Mrs Thatcher when she was Prime Minister. Admission to all clubs is by membership only.

Of more general interest are three of London's most intriguing small shops. John Lobb's at No. 9 was established in 1849 and has been 'bootmakers to the Crown' since 1911. Look inside the shop's small museum case for historical items such as the wooden last that was used for Queen Victoria's shoes. At No. 6 is James Lock & Co, the 'most famous hat shop in the world', which has provided headwear for national heroes such as Nelson and Wellington and where the bowler hat was invented. The picturesque early 19th-century premises of wine merchants Berry Brothers & Rudd are at No. 3, adjacent to a narrow alley leading to tiny Pickering Place where, between 1842 and 1845, the Republic of Texas kept a legation (diplomatic ministry).

🚪 28C3
✉️ Piccadilly
☎️ (020) 7734 4511; www.st-james-piccadilly.org
🕐 Daily Apr–Oct 8–7; Nov–Mar 9–6
🍴 Café (£)
🚇 Green Park, Piccadilly Circus
♿ Few; access via Jermyn Street
🎟️ Free
❓ Concerts, recitals: Mon, Wed, Fri at 1.10 (free). Evening concerts usually Thu, Fri, Sat at 7, 7.30 (expensive). Craft market Wed–Sat 11–7; antiques market Tue 10–6

🚪 28C2
🚇 Green Park

Above & left: *Lock & Co, where the Duke of Wellington bought the plumed hat that he wore at the Battle of Waterloo*

81D3
Dickens Inn (£)
Tower Hill
Free

ST. KATHARINE'S DOCK ✪✪

To experience London's huge dockland warehouses as they used to be without making the journey east, visit St. Katharine's Dock, conveniently close to the Tower of London. Here exotic items such as ostrich feathers, spices, teas, turtles and ivory (up to 22,000 tusks in a year) were once stored. The dock closed in 1968 and was developed to cater to the tourist trade with shops, restaurants and historic sailing ships at berth. The picturesque late 18th-century Dickens Inn pub-restaurant incorporates 17th-century timbers into its galleried frontage.

ST. PAUL'S CATHEDRAL (► 22, TOP TEN)

29F3
39 Walbrook
(020) 7283 4444
Mon–Thu 10–4, Fri 10–3
Sweetings (££) (► 96)
Bank, Cannon Street
Few
Free

ST. STEPHEN WALBROOK ✪✪

This is the Lord Mayor of London's parish church and is arguably the finest of all the City's churches. Built by Christopher Wren between 1672 and 1679, its dome was the first in England and was clearly a prototype for Wren's engineering *tour de force*, the dome of St. Paul's Cathedral. The church was beautifully restored between 1978 and 1987, with the original dark-wood fittings making a striking contrast to the gleaming white marble floor and the controversial giant white 'Camembert cheese' stone altarpiece, designed by Sir Henry Moore in 1972.

Above: *Unable to take large ships, St. Katharine's Dock was never a commercial success*
Right: *Trial run for St. Paul's: St Stephen Walbrook*

SCIENCE MUSEUM (► 23, TOP TEN)

Did you know ?

For centuries Southwark was the centre of London's forbidden pleasures. Because it lay just outside the City fathers' jurisdiction, venues such as bull-baiting and bear-baiting rings, cock-fighting pits, rowdy inns, brothels and gambling dens were all allowed to flourish. Theatres too were deemed to be unacceptable within the City, hence the location of the Globe and other famous Elizabethan playhouses.

SHAKESPEARE'S GLOBE EXHIBITION ✪✪

In May 1997 Shakespeare's circular wooden Globe Theatre was finally completed after 25 years hard work, the dream of American film and theatre director, the late Sam Wanamaker. Constructed according to contemporary late 16th-century techniques, it was the first thatched building to be erected in London since the Great Fire of 1666. The Globe Exhibition, telling the story behind this remarkable project, features a major exhibition on the world of Shakespeare and includes a theatrical tour.

✚ 29E3
✉ New Globe Walk, Bankside
☎ (020) 7902 1400; www.shakespeares-globe.org
◷ Daily: May–Sep 9–12, Oct–Apr 10–5. Closed 24, 25 Dec
🍴 Globe Café (£), Globe Restaurant (££)
Ⓜ Mansion House, Southwark
♿ Very good
💷 Expensive
❓ Guided tours. Theatre performances May–Sep
☎ (020) 77401 9919
(► 112)

Above: *Shakespeare's Globe Theatre*
Left: *The bizarre interior of the Sir John Soane's Museum*

SIR JOHN SOANE'S MUSEUM ✪✪✪

In terms of size and layout, this extraordinary labyrinthine museum is the most unusual art and antiquities collection in the capital. It was formerly the home of the designer and architect Sir John Soane (1753–1837) and has, according to the terms specified by Soane himself, been kept exactly in its original condition. Much of this magpie collection is arranged around a central court and is aided and abetted by false walls, alcoves, domes and skylights. Its treasures include masterpieces (cleverly hung on hinged panels which go flat to the wall to save space) by Turner, Canaletto and Hogarth (including the famous *Rake's Progress* series), a sarcophagus from the Valley of the Kings, a bizarre Gothic folly entitled the 'Monk's Parlour', plus sculptures and stone fragments galore.

✚ 29D3
✉ 13 Lincoln's Inn Fields
☎ (020) 7405 2107; www.soane.org
◷ Tue–Sat 10–5. Also first Tue of the month 6–9. Closed all public hols
🍴 Lamb pub (£) (► 97)
Ⓜ Holborn
♿ Most of ground floor accessible
💷 Free (charge for exhibitions)
❓ Excellent guided tour Sat 2.30 (moderate)

69

🗺 28C3
🍴 Many options available
🚇 Piccadilly Circus,
Tottenham Court Road,
Oxford Circus

*Soho's Chinatown is one
of the best places for
cheap and interesting
food in the capital*

🗺 29F3
✉ Cathedral Street
☎ (020) 7367 6700;
www.dswark.org/
cathedral
🕐 Mon–Fri 9–5, Sat 10–4,
Sun 10–6
🍴 Café/restaurant (£) in
cathedral refectory
🚇 London Bridge
♿ Good
✋ Moderate

🗺 28C2
✉ 27 St. James's Place
☎ (020) 7499 8620;
www.spencerhouse.co.uk
🕐 Sun 10.30–4.45. Closed
Jan, Aug
🚇 Green Park
♿ Very good 💰 Expensive
❓ No children under 10

SOHO ✪✪✪

Soho, bounded roughly by Oxford Street, Regent Street, Coventry Street/Leicester Square and Charing Cross Road, is central London's most cosmopolitan area. Over the centuries it has accommodated waves of French Huguenot, Italian, Greek and latterly Chinese immigrants, and artists too have long been drawn here, giving Soho its Bohemian reputation. In the 1960s and 1970s the area became notorious for sleaze, though a clean-up in the 1980s closed some of the worst establishments. Today the area is known for its many reasonably priced restaurants, its buzzing nightlife, and more recently, as a gay centre.

SOUTHWARK CATHEDRAL ✪

Often overlooked by visitors, Southwark Cathedral boasts one of the oldest and most interesting church interiors in the capital. Construction began in 1220 and was finished some 200 years later (though most of its exterior features were remodelled much later). The nave retains some original stonework and fascinating 15th-century bosses—one depicts the devil swallowing Judas Iscariot. There are several grand monuments, the most notable being to the area's most famous parishioner, William Shakespeare, who lived in Southwark from 1599 to 1611. His brother Edmund (died 1607) and other fellow dramatists are buried in the cathedral.

SPENCER HOUSE ✪✪

Built between 1756 and 1766 for Earl Spencer (an ancestor of the late Diana, Princess of Wales), Spencer House is London's finest surviving mid-18th century house. Indeed, it has been described as London's most magnificent private palace. After being completely restored at a cost of £16 million, it was opened to visitors in 1990. The one-hour guided tour takes in eight rooms featuring elegant gilded decorations and period paintings and furniture.

TATE BRITAIN AND TATE MODERN

In 2000 the Tate Gallery, one of London's great artistic institutions, split into two—Tate Britain and Tate Modern.

Tate Britain occupies the original Millbank site and retains its function as the showcase of British art from 1500 to the present. The national collection now fills Henry Tate's refurbished building, completed in 2001. It is impossible to say what will be on display at any one time as exhibits go in and out of storage and are also rotated to provincial Tate museums. However the highlight of the British collection is the Turner Bequest, comprising many of the finest works of J. M. W. Turner, regarded by many as Britain's greatest landscape painter. The Tate Britain has a superb collection of High Victorian and Pre-Raphaelite pictures and the controversial Turner Prize is staged annually here.

Tate Modern, housed in Sir Giles Gilbert Scott's formidable Bankside Power Station, on the South Bank of the Thames opposite St. Paul's, opened in summer 2000. It iwas not only the first major new museum in the capital for over a century but also one of the most important contemporary galleries in the world, devoted to art post-1900. Look out for works by Picasso, Matisse, Mondrian, Duchamp, Bacon, Rothko and Warhol.

Tate Britain
- 29D1
- Millbank
- (020) 7887 8000; recorded information (020) 7887 8008; www.tate.org.uk
- Daily 10–5.50
- Tate Café (£); Tate Britain Restaurant (£££) (020) 7887 8825
- Westminster
- Excellent
- Free (charge for exhibitions)
- Free guided tours Mon–Sat. Personal audio guide (free). Art Trolley activities for children (aged 5+) Sun 2–5. Shuttle service by bus and boat to Tate Modern

Tate Modern
- 29E3
- Bankside
- As above
- Daily 10–6 (Fri, Sat open until 10pm)
- Tate Café (£); Tate Restaurant (£££)
- Southwark
- Excellent
- Free
- Audio tours (inexpensive). Footbridge from St. Paul's Cathedral. Shuttle service by bus and boat to Tate Britain

Left: *The original Tate Gallery on Millbank, now Tate Britain*

THEATRE MUSEUM

An outpost of the Victoria & Albert Museum, this museum focuses on the performing arts from Shakespeare's day to the present. Displays embrace every aspect of theatre including opera, music hall, ballet, pantomime, the circus, puppetry and pop music. Opened in 1987, the Theatre Museum also exhibits props, costumes, programmes, posters, model theatres and tickets. Theatrical greats such as David Garrick and Sir John Gielgud are represented in portraits and there is an important exhibition on the history of West End theatres.

- 29D3
- Russell Street
- (020) 77943 4700; www.theatremuseu.org
- Tue–Sun 10–6
- Cafés and restaurants nearby (£–£££)
- Covent Garden
- Excellent Free
- Workshops; demonstrations

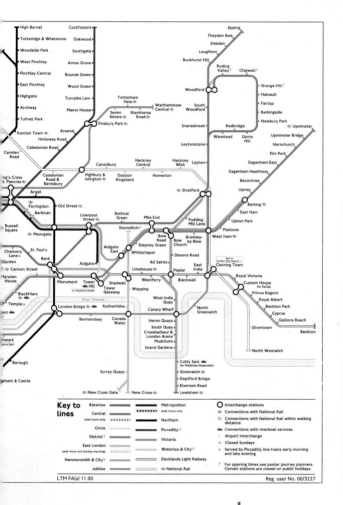

Key to lines

Bakerloo	Metropolitan	
Central	Northern	
Circle	Piccadilly †	
District †	Victoria	
East London	Waterloo & City †	
Hammersmith & City †	Docklands Light Railway	
Jubilee	National Rail	

○ Interchange stations
⇌ Connections with National Rail
⊕ Connections with National Rail within walking distance
⛴ Connections with riverboat services
✈ Airport interchange
★ Closed Sundays
▲ Served by Piccadilly line trains early morning and late evening
† For opening times see poster journey planners. Certain stations are closed on public holidays.

LTM FA(a) 11.00   Reg. user No. 00/3227

29F2

Tower Bridge Exhibition
- Tower Bridge
- (020) 7940 3985;
  www.towerbridge.org.uk
- Daily Apr–Sep 10–6.30;
  Oct–Mar 9.30–6. Last
  admission 1 hour
  before closing
- Butler's Wharf Chop
  House (£££) (➤ 92)
- Tower Hill, London
  Bridge
- Most areas accessible by
  lift
- Moderate
- Bridge lift information line
  (020) 7940 3984 or see
  website above

TOWER BRIDGE ✪✪✪

One of London's best-known landmarks, Tower Bridge was built between 1886 and 1894 and hailed as one of the greatest engineering feats of its day. It is basically a classic Victorian iron and steel structure, clad in stone to match the medieval appearance of its neighbour, the Tower of London. Until quite recently it was the last road bridge across the Thames before the river reaches the North Sea, and it remains London's only drawbridge. This function was to allow large ships to pass into the busy Upper Pool of London, which was a hive of warehouse activity in Victorian times. At its peak, its bascules were like yo-yos, up and down 50 times a day. Today they open on average around 18 times a week to allow tall ships, cruise ships and naval vessels through.

The structure now houses the **Tower Bridge Exhibition**, an informative multi-media exhibition that explains the history of the bridge. You can also step right into the bowels of the building to see the original Victorian engine rooms which were used to raise the bascules from 1894 to 1976. The high-level walkways, 43m (141ft) above the river, were designed to allow pedestrians to cross when the drawbridges were raised, and the views are unbeatable. Even from ground level Tower Bridge is one of the city's great vantage points.

TOWER OF LONDON (➤ 24, TOP TEN)

Did you know ?

Tower Bridge contains over 27,000 tons of bricks, enough to build around 350 detached houses. An average of 432 men worked for nearly 2,900 days on it, and the final cost was around £1.2 million. The bridge is 268m (292 yards) long from shore to shore and its drawbridges each weigh 1,000 tons.

Left: *Hitler planned to remove Nelson's Column from London to Berlin as a symbol of final victory*

Below left: *Tower Bridge, 'the most monumental example of extravagance in bridge construction in the world'*

TRAFALGAR SQUARE ✪✪✪

This is the geographical and symbolic centre of London; all road distances are measured from here and, at its middle, Nelson's Column is one of London's most potent symbols. The buildings of South Africa House, Canada House and the National Gallery line three sides of the square, while the fourth opens to Whitehall. The square takes its name from the Battle of Trafalgar in 1805, during which Admiral Nelson, Britain's greatest naval hero, commanded his fleet to the famous victory against Franco-Spanish forces. Nelson was killed during the battle and the column, 57m (187ft) high, was erected between 1839 and 1842.

The church on the square, with its landmark tower dramatically floodlit by night, is **St. Martin-in-the-Fields**, built in 1726 by James Gibbs. This handsome building is famous for concerts and is also a thriving community centre with a social care unit and several minor visitor attractions. Above ground it hosts a daily clothes and crafts market, while its famous crypt houses an art gallery, the London Brass Rubbing Centre, gift shops and the excellent Café-in-the-Crypt.

VICTORIA AND ALBERT MUSEUM (► 25, TOP TEN)

🚩 29D3

St. Martin-in-the-Fields

✉ Trafalgar Square

☎ General enquiries (020) 7766 1100; concert enquiries (020) 7839 8362; www.stmartin-in-the-fields.org

🕐 Church Mon–Sat 8–6.30, Sun 8–7.30. Crypt brass rubbing centre Mon–Wed 10–7, Thu–Sat 10–10, Sun 12–7. Concerts Mon, Tue, Fri at 1pm. Candlelit concerts of baroque music most Thu–Sat 7.30

🍴 Café-in-the-Crypt (£)

Ⓒ Charing Cross, Leicester Square

♿ Ramp to church, no wheelchair access to café

💰 Free. Lunchtime concerts free, evening concerts expensive

🔲 28B3
✉ Hertford House,
Manchester Square
☎ (020) 7563 9500;
www.wallace-
collection.org
🕐 Daily 10–5
🍴 Wallace Restaurant (££)
Ⓔ Bond Street
♿ All areas accessible; no
electric wheelchairs
Ⓥ Free
❓ Free guided tours

WALLACE COLLECTION ✪✪✪

This is one of the capital's hidden gems, the perfect antidote to the bustle of nearby Oxford Street. The collection is housed in the peaceful surroundings of a small stately home and you can enjoy some of London's finest works of art while clocks tick gently, secure in the knowledge that there will be only a handful of fellow visitors to disturb your concentration.

The predominant theme of the collection, the legacy of the inveterate 19th-century collector, Sir Richard Wallace, is French 18th-century art. Downstairs, the André Boulle furniture (including pieces made for the Palace of Versailles), is truly staggering, both in opulence and sheer bulk. Alongside is the best museum collection of Sèvres porcelain in the world. Less well known is the Wallace's magnificent collection of arms and armour—arguably the equal of that in the Tower of London. Upstairs in the picture galleries the Gallic theme continues. The most notable exception is the famous Gallery 22, where, among works by Rubens, Rembrandt, Claude and Velázquez, the star exhibits are the *Laughing Cavalier* by Frans Hals and *Perseus and Andromeda* by Titian.

WESTMINSTER ABBEY (▶ 26, TOP TEN)

🔲 28C2
✉ Victoria Street
☎ (020) 7798 9055;
www.westminster
cathedral.org.uk
🕐 Mon–Fri 7–7, Sat, Sun
8–7. Campanile Mar–Nov
daily 9.30–12.30, 1–5;
Dec–Feb Thu–Sun only
Ⓔ Victoria
♿ Accessible to
wheelchairs
Ⓥ Cathedral free; campanile
moderate

WESTMINSTER CATHEDRAL ✪

Not to be confused with the more illustrious abbey of the same name, Westminster Cathedral is London's principal Roman Catholic church. Its foundation is relatively modern, being built between 1896 and 1903. The slim, handsome Byzantine campanile (accessible by lift) is one of the capital's lesser-known landmarks, towering some 83m (272ft) high and offering great views over central London. The cathedral interior is famous for some of the finest and most varied marble-work in the country, though it has never been completed (owing to lack of funds) and much of the huge nave ceiling still shows bare brickwork.

Westminster Cathedral is a brick masterpiece with 12.5 million in all and no steel reinforcements

True Brit: 10 Downing Street (above) and Guardsman at Horse Guards (left)

WHITEHALL

Whitehall has been the country's principal corridor of power since the early 18th century. The epicentre is Downing Street, home to the Prime Minister and to the Chancellor of the Exchequer, while to north and south are various grey and sober buildings that house the country's top civil servants and ministries. Just south of Downing Street is the Cenotaph, the national memorial to the dead of the two World Wars. The street was named after Henry VIII's Whitehall Palace, which burned down in 1698, leaving the Banqueting House (► 33) as the sole surviving building above ground. Opposite here is Horse Guards, the historic, official entrance to the royal palaces, still guarded by two mounted troopers and a good place to watch one of London's least fussy, least crowded guard-changing ceremonies.

🚇 29D2

🕐 No public access to Downing Street

🍴 Café-in-the-Crypt (£), (► 92)

🚉 South end Westminster; north end Charing Cross

❓ Horse Guards guard changes 11am Mon–Sat, 10am Sun; ceremonial dismounting and inspection daily at 4. National Remembrance Service held at the Cenotaph at 11am on Sun nearest 11 Nov

WINSTON CHURCHILL'S BRITAIN AT WAR

Sheltered appropriately deep beneath the arches of London Bridge, this is an evocative museum of what it was like to live in the capital during the dark and dangerous period of World War II, and particularly during the Blitz of 1940–41. Aside from examining a huge number of well-displayed original period objects, you can sit in an air-raid shelter or walk through an eerily authentic bombed-out building. Older visitors will enjoy the bitter-sweet nostalgia of such displays as life on the Home Front, evacuation, movie news and re-created shopfronts, while younger ones will enjoy the drama without experiencing the trauma of those momentous years.

🚇 29F2

✉ 64–6 Tooley Street

☎ (020) 7403 3171; www.britainatwar.co.uk

🕐 Daily 10–5.30 (Oct–Mar 4.30)

🍴 Butler's Wharf Chop House (£££), 36E Shad Thames (► 92)

🚉 London Bridge

♿ Excellent

💷 Expensive

Outer London & Beyond

When the crowds and noise of central London begin to make you wonder if you made the right choice by taking a city holiday, it's time to head out of town: Fortunately you don't have to go far before the whole atmosphere changes.

The easiest and most popular excursion is downriver to Greenwich, full of history, good shopping and restaurants. Upriver lie Hampton Court and Kew Gardens. Each makes a glorious sunny summer's day out, but don't try to combine the two—there is far too much to see. Return visitors to London should seek out the low-key but highly enjoyable pleasures of riverside Richmond and Twickenham.

If you have time to leave the metropolis for a day or two, Bath is an urban dream; Oxford and Cambridge are fascinating for their universities; while Windsor Castle is a treat for lovers of history and royalty.

> '*Thy Forests, Windsor!*
> *and thy green Retreats.*
> *At once the Monarch's and*
> *the Muse's Seats*'
>
> ALEXANDER POPE,
> *Windsor-Forest*, 1713

Left: *The Cutty Sark in Maritime Greenwich*

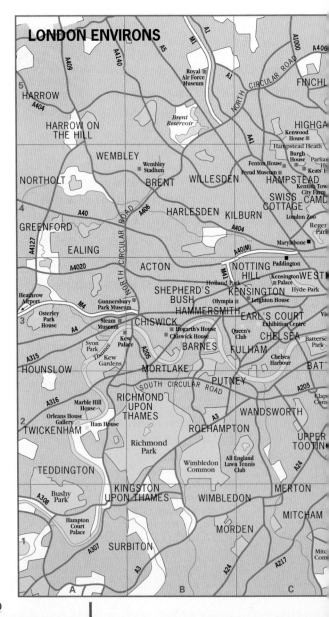

LONDON ENVIRONS

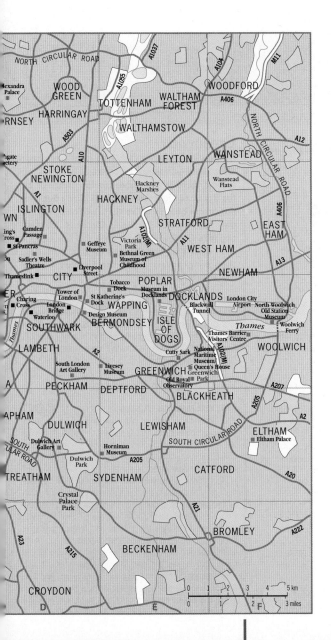

Tourist Information Office

- ✉ 2 Cutty Sark Gardens
- ☎ 0870 608 2000
- 🕐 Daily 10–5
- ❓ Guided walking tours depart daily 12.15, 2.15
  ☎ (020) 8858 6169

The Royal Naval College, designed by Sir Christopher Wren as a hospital for naval pensioners

- ✚ 81E3
- ✉ Greenwich Park
- ☎ (020) 8312 6565; 0870 780 4552;
  www.nmm.ac.uk
- 🕐 Sep–Jun daily 1–5, Jul–Aug daily 10–6. Closed 24–26 Dec
- 🍴 The Regatta Café (£), National Maritime Museum (▶ 98)
- 🚢 Greenwich Pier
- 🚇 DLR to Cutty Sark
- 🚆 Greenwich from London Bridge
- ♿ Excellent
- Free

Greenwich

Greenwich (pronounced Gren-itch) lies some 10km (6 miles) east of the centre of London. You can get there by train from London Bridge or on the Dockland Light Railway (DLR) direct. But why not take a boat to arrive the traditional way, or perhaps the DLR to Island Gardens, directly opposite Greenwich. From here you can enjoy a river view that has changed little in centuries, then simply walk under the Thames via the Greenwich Foot Tunnel.

Though suffering from heavy traffic and summer crowds, Greenwich retains something of a village atmosphere with lots of interesting small shops, a throbbing market, an abundance of historic attractions and one of London's finest parks. Greenwich is also the site of the Millennium Dome, the focal point of Britain's millennium celebrations.

What to See in Greenwich

NATIONAL MARITIME MUSEUM   ✪✪✪

The National Maritime Museum was give a major makeover to celebrate the Millennium and while it may be the world's largest and most important maritime museum, it also takes a sufficiently broad view that it is appealing to even the most confirmed land lubber.

At its heart is the Neptune Court, a dramatic glassed-over courtyard holding the museum's largest objects, such as the carved and gilded state barge made for Frederick, Prince of Wales, in 1732. Off here are 15 or so major galleries that explain the history and role of maritime Greenwich, Britain as a once-great sea power and more worldwide topics such ocean exploration. Some of the finest ship models and great maritime paintings are also here. Younger visitors should head for All Hands and The Bridge, two hands-on galleries for budding seafarers. Britain's greatest naval hero, Admiral Lord Nelson, gets lots of gallery space covering his career and private life.

ROYAL OBSERVATORY ✪✪

The Royal Observatory was founded in 1675 by Charles II to find out the 'so-much desired longitude of places for perfecting the art of (sea) navigation'. Set high on a mound in Greenwich Park, and commanding a splendid view (even today), it was designed by Sir Christopher Wren and functioned as Britain's principal observatory until 1945. Today it is a museum that tells the history of the observatory and offers a crash course in the measurement of time and astronomy. This is not an easy subject to grasp, but displays are well explained and feature some beautiful historical instruments. There is also a fascinating camera obscura to visit. The prime attraction for most visitors, however, is to be photographed standing astride the 0° longitude line (which passes right through the observatory) with one foot in the eastern hemisphere and one foot in the western hemisphere.

🕂 81E3
✉ Greenwich Park
☎ 020 8312 6565;
www.nmm.ac.uk
🕐 Sep–Jun daily 10–5,
Jul–Aug daily 10–6.
Closed 24–26 Dec
🍴 The Regatta Café (£),
National Maritime
Museum (➤ 98)
🚢 River boat to Greenwich
Pier
Ⓡ DLR to Cutty Sark
🚆 Greenwich from London
Bridge
♿ Not all the buildings are
fully accessible. Special
access days can be
arranged
✋ Free

The distinctive dome of the Royal Observatory

QUEEN'S HOUSE ✪✪

This exquisite miniature palace is set at the heart of Greenwich's historic riverfront complex and was the very first classical-style building in England, begun in 1616. It was designed by Inigo Jones. The queen in question was originally Anne of Denmark, wife of James I, though by the time of completion in 1635 she had died and Henrietta Maria, wife of Charles I, assumed tenancy.

🕂 81E3
✉ Greenwich Park
☎ (020) 8312 6565;
www.nmm.ac.uk
🕐 Daily 10–5. Closed 24–26
Dec
🍴 The Regatta Café (£),
National Maritime
Museum (➤ 98)
🚢 Greenwich Pier
Ⓡ DLR to Cutty Sark
🚆 Greenwich from London
Bridge
♿ Partial access. Special
access days can be
arranged
✋ Free

Did you know ?

Contrary to popular legend, Admiral Lord Nelson never wore an eye patch, though he did have a special hat (on display in Westminster Abbey's Undercroft Museum) to shade the eye he injured at the Battle of Calvi. The bullet-holed jacket and blood-stained clothing that Nelson wore at the Battle of Trafalgar is in the Maritime London Gallery.

Around Greenwich

Distance
Approximately 3km (2 miles)

Time
2–4 hours, depending on visits

Start point
⊞ 40A1
Greenwich Pier
🚤 River boat to Greenwich Pier
Ⓓ DLR to Island Gardens, then foot tunnel.
🚆 Greenwich from London Bridge

End point
⊞ 40A1
Old Royal Naval College (next to Greenwich Pier)

Lunch
A picnic in the park

Cutty Sark
☎ (020) 8858 3445
🕙 Daily 10–5
💷 Moderate

Old Royal Naval College and Chapel
☎ (020) 8269 4747
🕙 Daily 10–5
💷 Free

The view from the Observatory across to Docklands

The maritime heritage of Greenwich is immediately apparent even before you land at Greenwich Pier, where tall masts and rigging signpost the *Cutty Sark*. Launched in 1869, this is the last surviving British sailing clipper designed to carry cargoes between Britain and the Orient. In 1871 she broke the world record for sailings between London and China, completing the trip in 107 days, and is famous for her collection of ships' figureheads.

Pick up a map from the tourist office in Cutty Sark Gardens then walk up Greenwich Church Street and go through the market (➤ 109) to emerge on King William Walk. Turn right and enter Greenwich Park.

Follow any of the paths that lead up to the Old Royal Observatory (➤ 83) from where you can enjoy one of London's finest views.

Continue along Blackheath Avenue.

Turn left towards the bandstand, the lovely park gardens and the adjacent wilderness area where deer have been resident for centuries.

*Walk back downhill and exit the park near the boating pond into Park Row, then turn left into Romney Road to the entrance to the **Old Royal Naval College and Chapel**.*

This majestic baroque complex was built by Sir Christopher Wren between 1694 and 1745 as a home for Royal Naval Pensioners. They left here in 1869 and until recently the building was used as a Royal Naval College.

What to See around Outer London

HAMPTON COURT PALACE ✪✪✪

Work on Hampton Court Palace began in 1514 under the tenure of Henry VIII's Lord Chancellor, Cardinal Wolsey. By 1528, however, Wolsey had fallen from favour and Henry had acquired it for himself. He built it up to be the most lavish palace in England where he fêted European royalty and spent five of his six honeymoons. William III and Mary II commissioned Sir Christopher Wren to remodel the apartments and to give the palace much of its present-day appearance. George II was the last monarch to use Hampton Court.

For most visitors the Tudor survivals are still the palace highlights; the great gatehouse and a magnificent astronomical clock, the capacious Tudor Kitchens stocked with contemporary foods and utensils, and fires ablaze all year round, the sumptuous centrepiece Great Hall and the Chapel Royal with its breathtaking ceiling. The King's Apartments (built by William III) are among the finest baroque state apartments in the world and the Wolsey Rooms hold a fine Renaissance picture gallery, though the palace's greatest artwork, *Triumphs of Caesar* by Mantegna, is in the orangery. The gardens, planted in the late 17th century, are glorious and include the ever-popular maze, the Great Vine (England's largest) and the Royal Tennis Court. The latter was built in 1626 and real tennis (a hybrid of squash and lawn tennis) is still played here regularly.

✚ 80A1

✉ Hampton Court

☎ 0870 753 7777; 0870 752 7777; www.hrp.org.uk

🕓 Daily

🍴 Garden café (£) and restaurant (££)

🚆 Train from Waterloo direct to Hampton Court. Boat from Westminster, Richmond or Kew (summer only)

🚌 111, 216, 411, 416, 451, 461, 513, 726, R68

♿ Excellent

💷 All-inclusive ticket to palace and gardens very expensive. Maze only moderate. Gardens moderate

Above: Hampton Court Palace is famous for its gardens and holds a flower show every July

KEW GARDENS
(ROYAL BOTANIC GARDENS)

★★★

Founded in the late 18th century, Kew Gardens, a huge park of almost 122ha (300 acres), holds a marvellous collection of plants, trees and flowers from every corner of the globe. Most of the species are grown outdoors, but huge glass and wrought iron greenhouses replicate exotic climes—from rainforest, to swamp, to desert. The most spectacular of these is the curvy Palm House, built between 1844 and 1848. The Temperate House was the world's largest greenhouse when built in 1899 and contains a Chilean Wine Palm some 18m (60ft) tall and over 150 years old. The Princess of Wales Conservatory is a favourite for its giant water-lily pads, and the exhibition Evolution is a high-tech exploration of the story of the planet to date.

Reminders of the gardens' early royal patronage are provided by tiny Kew Palace (summer home of George III 1802–18), Queen Charlotte's Cottage and the Queen's Garden. Also in the gardens are notable follies, including Kew's distinctive pagoda, plus museums and galleries.

80A3

☎ (020) 8940 1171; www.kew.org

🕙 Daily from 9.30. Closes approx. 5.30 winter, 7.30 summer. Closed 25 Dec, 1 Jan

🍴 Café (£), restaurant (£–££)

🚇 Kew Gardens. Riverboat to Kew Pier from Westminster and Richmond (summer only)

♿ All areas except Marianne North gallery accessible

💷 Expensive

❓ Kew Explorer hop-on hop-off land train (moderate)

Above: *Kew Gardens' greenhouses replicate even the driest of climates*

Right: *The Pagoda built in 1761 towers 50m (164ft) high; sadly it is not open to the public*

Opposite: *Ham House features one of the finest Stuart interiors in the country and lovely gardens*

RICHMOND AND TWICKENHAM ✪✪✪

These adjoining riverside suburbs just west of town make up one of London's most charming and bucolic districts. From Richmond station turn left to walk along George Street. Off here to the right is a lovely village green. Return to George Street and continue to Richmond Bridge and the impressive new classical-style riverside development. To visit Richmond Park take bus 371 and get off at the Royal Star & Garter; here you can enjoy the magnificent view down on to the river that has been painted by numerous artists, including J. M. W. Turner.

Richmond Park, London's largest royal park and one of its wildest, with herds of deer, makes an ideal place for a picnic. If you want to explore it properly consider hiring a bicycle. As an alternative to the park, follow the towpath along the river from Richmond Bridge (it's possible to cycle along here) and after around 30 minutes you will reach **Ham House**. This is an outstanding 17th-century house that has been refurbished to its former glory.

To get to Twickenham (on the opposite side of the river) walk back a short way to the Hammerton Ferry and cross to **Marble Hill House**, a lovely Palladian villa built for a mistress of George II in the early 1720s. A short walk further on is **Orleans House Gallery** where temporary art exhibitions are staged in a beautiful baroque octagon room. To return to Richmond, walk up Orleans Road and catch any one of several buses that run along the Richmond Road.

✚ 80A2

ℹ Old Town Hall, Richmond
☎ (020) 8940 9125
🕐 Mon–Sat 10–5, also Sun May–Sep only 10.30–1.30

Ham House

✉ Ham Street, Ham
☎ (020) 8940 1950
🕐 House: Apr–Oct Sat–Wed 1–5. Gardens: all year Sat–Wed 11–6
💷 Expensive

Marble Hill House

✉ Richmond Road, Twickenham
☎ (020) 8892 5115
🕐 Apr–Oct Sat 10–2, Sun and public hols 10–5
💷 Moderate

Orleans House Gallery

✉ Riverside, Twickenham
☎ (020) 8831 6000
🕐 Tue–Sat 1–5.30, Sun 2–5.30, (4.30 Oct–Mar)
💷 Free

Excursions away from London

BATH ✪✪✪

Designated as a UNESCO World Heritage Site, the honey-coloured city of Bath was developed as a fashionable spa in the 18th century and is a perfect example of a Georgian town. It was the **Roman Baths** that first established the city and, still remarkably complete, they form the most impressive Roman remains in Britain. Adjacent is another 'must-see' site, Bath Abbey, dating mostly from the 16th century. A short walk away is the Royal Crescent, built between 1767 and 1774. This glorious terrace of 30 classically inspired three-storey houses in glowing golden Bath stone is often claimed to be the most majestic street in Britain.

Just outside Bath, at Claverton, is the excellent **American Museum**, which features 15 authentically re-created 17th- to 19th-century rooms.

CAMBRIDGE ✪✪✪

Cambridge is famous for its university, one of the oldest and most prestigious in Britain, alongside Oxford. The oldest college is Peterhouse, founded in 1284, but the most noted college is King's, established in 1441 and renowned for its magnificent medieval architecture and almost heavenly choir. Outstanding among the other 31 colleges are Queen's, Trinity, Magdalene, St. John's, Clare, Jesus and Emmanuel. All the colleges now admit men and women, but Magdalene has only done this since 1988.

The Backs is a strip of grassy meadow-cum-lawns between the rear of the colleges and the River Cam. It is a fine venue for a picnic and is a good place for college viewing. Spanning the Cam are two famous bridges: the Bridge of Sighs, a copy of the famous Venetian bridge; and the Mathematical Bridge, a wooden crossing now bolted together but originally assembled without a single metal fixing. The town's principal museum is the **Fitzwilliam Museum**, with outstanding collections of paintings, antiquities, ceramics and armour.

Tourist Information Centre
- ✉ Abbey Church Yard
- ☎ Personal callers, or fax (01225) 477221; www.visitbath.co.uk
- 🕐 Mon–Sat 9.30–6 (5 in winter), Sun 10–4

Roman Baths
- ✉ Stall Street
- ☎ (01225) 477785; www.romanbaths.co.uk
- 🕐 Mar–Jun, Sep–Oct 9–6; rest of year 9.30–5.30
- 💵 Expensive

American Museum
- ✉ Claverton Manor, Bath
- ☎ (01225) 460503; www.americanmuseum.org
- 🕐 Mid-Mar to Oct Tue–Sun 12–5.30
- 💵 Moderate

Right: *Elegant Georgian façades: The Circus, Bath*

Tourist Information Centre
- ✉ Wheeler Street
- ☎ 0906 586256 (premium rate)
- 🕐 Oct–Mar Mon–Fri 10–5.30, Sat 10–5; Apr–Sep also Sun and BH Mon 11–4

Fitzwilliam Museum
- ✉ Trumpington Street
- ☎ (01223) 332900; www.fitzmuseum.com.ac.uk
- 🕐 Tue–Sat 10–5, Sun 12–5. Closed Mon (except Easter Mon and Spring public hol Mon), Good Fri
- 💵 Free
- ❓ Music Sun 1.15

Around Oxford

Start from the tourist information centre (➤ 90), where you can pick up maps and leaflets.

Turn right into St. Aldate's Street and enter Christ Church college through the War Memorial Garden. Exit left from the gate by the Picture Gallery into Oriel Square, named after the college on the right-hand side. Visit the college grounds then continue up Oriel Street to High Street, where you emerge opposite the splendid 17th-century portico of the University Church of St. Mary the Virgin. Visit the church, then leave from the rear entrance into Radcliffe Square.

On your left is Brasenose College, while in the middle of the square is the Radcliffe Camera, built in 1749 and now part of the **Bodleian Library**. Join a tour to see the magnificent Duke Humfrey's Library and Divinity School, a masterpiece of Gothic architecture.

Go through Schools Quad and turn left at the far end.

The domed **Sheldonian Theatre** ahead was designed by Sir Christopher Wren between 1663 and 1669. Climb to the top for a view of Oxford's 'dreaming spires'.

Leave the Sheldonian and walk straight ahead, crossing Catte Street, and beneath Oxford's very own Bridge of Sighs across Queen's Lane.

For a pub lunch turn immediately left into St. Helen's Passage and follow it to the famous Turf Tavern.

Return to New College Lane and follow this around to New College, noting the splendid gargoyles and grotesques on the wall. Leaving New College, Queen's Lane takes you between Queen's College (right) and St. Edmund Hall (also a college, left).

Turn right on to the High Street and walk a little further to Magdalen College (pronounced 'Mordlin'), with luck in time to attend the famous Evensong performance (generally at 6pm, but check with the tourist information centre).

Distance
Approx 5km (3 miles)

Time
4–6 hours depending on which colleges are open

Start point
Tourist information centre

End point
Magdalen College

Lunch
Turf Tavern (£)
✉ 4 Bath Place, via St. Helen's Passage

Bodleian Library
✉ Broad Street
☎ (01865) 277000
🕐 Guided tours mid-Mar to Oct Mon–Fri 10.30, 11.30, 2, 3; Sat 10.30, 11.30; Nov to mid-Mar Mon–Fri 2, 3; Sat 10.30, 11.30
👤 Moderate
♿ Wheelchair access ground floor only; phone in advance

Sheldonian Theatre
✉ Broad Street
☎ (01865) 277299
🕐 Mon–Sat 10–12.30, 2–4.30 (3.30 in winter). All times subject to functions
👤 Cheap
❓ To find out which colleges are open visit www.ox.ca.uk and follow the Visitors link

OXFORD ✪✪✪

Oxford is synonymous with its university, the oldest in Britain. The most outstanding colleges are Christ Church, New College and Magdalen. Oxford also has plenty of non-university attractions, including the **Ashmolean Museum**, home to one of Britain's finest provincial collections, and the Pitt-Rivers Museum, an extraordinary and delightfully old-fashioned Victorian ethnographic treasure-trove. The charming Covered Market selling food and clothing, plus all sorts of other things, is also worth a visit.

WINDSOR ✪✪✪

Windsor is famous above all for its spectacularly sited **castle**, which (like the Tower of London) dates back to the time of William the Conqueror and has been continuously occupied since the 11th century. It has been enlarged and remodelled many times, though it took on its basic present shape in the 12th and 14th centuries. The castle is one of the three official residences of the Sovereign (the others are Buckingham Palace and Holyrood House, Edinburgh) and as such is in regular working use. In 1992 it suffered significant fire damage, but all areas have since been fully repaired and restored.

The most impressive of all the castle buildings is St. George's Chapel, a masterpiece of English Gothic architecture, completed in 1511. Ten monarchs lie here, including Henry VIII and Charles I. The state apartments are hung with works from the Royal Collection, though the most startling exhibit is Queen Mary's Doll's House. Made in 1921 for the consort to King George V, it was designed in meticulous detail at one-twelfth life-size with working plumbing and lifts, and miniature paintings and books donated by eminent writers and artists of the day.

Windsor town is a busy shopping centre but you can escape the crowds by exploring Windsor Park, a perfect place for a picnic. Close by, Legoland (➤ 111) makes a great day out for young children.

Tourist Information Centre
✉ 15–16 Broad Street
☎ (01865) 726871
🕐 Mon–Sat 9.30–5, Sun 10–3.30 (closed Sun in winter)

Ashmolean Museum
✉ Beaumont Street
☎ (01865) 278000
🕐 Tue–Sat 10–5, Sun 12–5
✋ Free

Tourist Information Centre
✉ 24 High Street
☎ (01753) 743900
🕐 Mon–Fri, Sun 10–4, Sat 10–5. Extended hours in summer

Windsor Castle
✉ Entrance on Castle Hill
☎ (020) 7766 7304; 24-hour recorded information (01753) 831118
🕐 Daily Mar–Oct 9.45–5.15 (last admission 4); Nov–Feb 9.45–4.15 (last admission 3). St. George's Chapel open Mon–Sat; services only on Sun. Castle/apartments closed on or around 25, 27 Mar; 24 Apr; 11–14 Jun
✋ Very expensive

Henry VIII's Gate, the main entrance to Windsor Castle; the famous king is also buried here

Where To...

Eat and Drink	92–99
Stay	100–103
Shop	104–109
Take the Children	110–111
Be Entertained	112–115

Above: *At the Tower of London*
Right: *Sherlock Holmes' fictitious residence*

Central London

Price rating

Approximate price for a three-course meal per person, excluding drinks:

£ = under £25
££ = £25–£35
£££ = over £35

Opting for the *prix fixe* menu (or set meal) at lunch time usually means prices are dramatically reduced – perhaps even halved.

Booking is essential for all higher-priced restaurants. Many of the places featured here are London's busiest restaurants—book as soon as you arrive in the capital, if not before. Smart casual dress is the norm (and often required) in more expensive places.

Spoiled for choice

London has over 6,000 restaurants, 3,000 cafés and bars and 5,000 pubs serving food from over 50 different countries. If you want more recommendations than we have space for on the next few pages, then buy a copy of the excellent, annually updated *Time Out London Eating and Drinking* guide and also see the official London Tourist Board website www.visitlondon.com section on eating out. Beware, however, the latter is not updated as often as it should be.

Alastair Little (Soho) (£££)

Distinctive minimalist décor and fresh, light Modern European cooking from one of London's star chefs are the hallmarks of this famous Soho eatery. Book well in advance.

✉ **49 Frith Street, Soho** ☎ **(020) 7734 5183** ⏰ **Mon–Fri lunch, Mon–Sat dinner. Closed Sun** 🚇 **Leicester Square, Tottenham Court Road**

Al Bustan (£££)

The name means garden in Arabic and greenery abounds in this classy, formal Lebanese restaurant. The food is authentic and very tasty.

✉ **68 Old Brompton Road** ☎ **(020) 7584 5805** ⏰ **Daily 12–10.30** 🚇 **South Kensington**

Bibendum (£££)

The rich, robust Modern European cooking here rarely disappoints. It complements the brilliant Michelin art deco setting. Very popular so book well in advance.

✉ **Michelin House, 81 Fulham Road, SW3** ☎ **(020) 7581 5817** ⏰ **Daily lunch, dinner** 🚇 **South Kensington**

Bluebird (£££)

This King's Road 'Gastrodome' comprises an alfresco café, a lively flower market and excellent food shop, while the first floor is home to Bluebird restaurant which serves an eclectic range of Modern European cuisine. The Bluebird bar serves cutting edge cocktails and hosts DJs on Friday and Saturday evenings.

✉ **350 King's Road, Chelsea** ☎ **(020) 7559 1000** ⏰ **Daily lunch, dinner** 🚇 **Sloane Square then** 🚌 **19, 22**

Blues Bistro & Bar (£–££)

Trendy but not intimidating, with a small dining room, serving globally inspired contemporary classic dishes.

✉ **42–43 Dean Street** ☎ **(020) 7494 1966** ⏰ **Mon–Fri lunch, dinner, Sat dinner** 🚇 **Leicester Square**

Butler's Wharf Chop House (£–££)

Britannia rules the riverfront here with the very best of traditional and Modern British cuisine. Lovely dining room, try to book a table with a view of Tower Bridge.

✉ **Butler's Wharf Building, 36E Shad Thames** ☎ **(020) 7403 3403** ⏰ **Mon–Sat lunch, dinner; Sun brunch** 🚇 **Tower Hill, London Bridge**

Café-in-the-Crypt (£)

Dive beneath the Church of St. Martin-in-the-Fields to find this oasis of calm. Good salads, soups, sandwiches and light meals.

✉ **Duncannon Street (Trafalgar Square)** ☎ **(020) 7839 4342** ⏰ **Mon–Wed 10–8, Thu–Sat 10–11, Sun 12–8** 🚇 **Charing Cross, Leicester Square**

Café Pacifico (£–££)

This long-established Tex-Mex London institution is a cut above the average.

✉ **5 Langley Street** ☎ **(020) 7379 7728** ⏰ **Daily, 12–11.45pm (Sun 10.45pm)** 🚇 **Covent Garden**

The Capital (£££)

Some of the best *haute cuisine* in town, expertly served in a decorous and elegant setting.

✉ **22–4 Basil Street, Knightsbridge** ☎ **(020) 7589 5171** ⏰ **Daily lunch, dinner** 🚇 **Knightsbridge**

Le Caprice (£££)

It may be famous as the place where celebrities eat, but mortals also receive star treatment, and the food is excellent. Modern European cuisine in a setting of timeless classic décor.

✉ Arlington House, Arlington Street ☎ (020) 7629 2239
🕐 Daily lunch, dinner
🚇 Green Park

Chez Bruce (££–£££)

Worth the journey out to this very attractive informal dining room on Wandsworth Common to sample a menu of interesting combinations, based upon classical and regional French cuisine but also influenced by Mediterranean flavours.

✉ 2 Bellevue Road ☎ (020) 8672 0014 🕐 Daily lunch, dinner 🚇 Balham
🚉 Wandsworth Common

Angela Hartnett at the Connaught (£££)

Discreet, reserved and old-fashioned in the best sense, the classic cooking here, which gives a nod to British and Italian influences, is impeccable. Angela Hartnett learned her trade with Gordon Ramsay and seems destined for similar stardom.

✉ Carlos Place ☎ (020) 7499 7070 🕐 Daily lunch, dinner
🚇 Bond Street

L'Escargot, Marco Pierre White (ground floor ££), The Picasso Room (first floor £££)

This famous Soho establishment has been around since 1927. Recently revived by super chef Marco Pierre White, it is back to its best with spot-on French/Mediterranean cooking.

✉ 48 Greek Street ☎ (020) 7437 2679 🕐 Ground floor lunch Mon–Fri, dinner Mon–Sat; Picasso Room lunch Tue–Fri, dinner Tue–Sat 🚇 Tottenham Court Road

Floridita (££)

Terence Conran brings Cuba to W1. The food is Cuban and Latin American, but Floridita is as much about cigars (separate bar), hot rhythms (bands flown over from Havana), daiquiris and late-night clubbing, as the dining experience.

✉ 100 Wardour Street ☎ (020) 7314 4000 🕐 Mon–Wed 5.30–2, Thu–Sat 5.30–3
🚇 Piccadilly Circus

Gay Hussar (££)

London's most famous East European restaurant has been going strong for over 45 years thanks largely to its good-value Hungarian cooking.

✉ 2 Greek Street ☎ (020) 7437 0973 🕐 Daily lunch, Mon–Sat dinner 🚇 Tottenham Court Road

Gordon Ramsay (£££)

One of London's finest chefs (earning three Michelin stars). His restaurant serves some of the best modern French and haute cuisine in the country. Book weeks in advance.

✉ 68 Royal Hospital Road ☎ (020) 7352 4441 🕐 Daily lunch, Mon–Fri dinner
🚇 Sloane Square

Greenhouse (£££)

Inventive modern British cooking in a delightful garden effect restaurant. One of London's rising stars

✉ 27a Hay's Mews ☎ (020) 7499 3331 🕐 Mon–Fri lunch, Mon–Sat dinner 🚇 Green Park, Hyde Park Corner

Imperial China (£)

One of Chinatown's most attractive restaurants. The big draw is *dim sum*, though the full menu also proves good value.

✉ White Bear Yard, 25a Lisle Street ☎ (020) 7734 3388
🕐 Mon–Sat 12–11.45pm, Sun 11–11 🚇 Leicester Square

Afternoon Tea

If you want to take afternoon tea in style try one of the following hotels: the Ritz, the Savoy, the Lanesborough, the Waldorf Hilton, Brown's Hotel, Claridge's or the Dorchester. It's an expensive experience, but one you'll hopefully long treasure. Dress smartly (jacket and tie for men is the nominal code) and skip lunch beforehand! Other options (cheaper but still very classy) include Fortnum & Mason and the Wolseley.

Chain Eating

There are a number of restaurant chains in London that provide inexpensive food of a consistently reasonable standard. Probably the best is Pizza Express, with flagship branches at King's Road, Chelsea and at Dean Street, which is famous for its jazz. Other good value café-brasserie options are Giraffe, Pâtisserie Valerie, Carluccio's Caffé.

The Ivy (£££)

One of London's most popular restaurants (book weeks ahead), this is a lively place where the modern European cooking is special.

✉ 1 West Street, Covent Garden ☎ (020) 7836 4751 🍴 Daily lunch, dinner 🚇 Leicester Square, Covent Garden

Jason's Restaurant (£££)

This attractive popular restaurant beside the Grand Union Canal in Little Venice serves excellent modern European cuisine.

✉ Opposite 60 Blomfield Road, Maida Vale ☎ (020) 7286 6752 🍴 Daily lunch, Mon–Sat dinner 🚇 Warwick Avenue

Joe Allen (££)

The classic mainstream American food is hit-and-miss here, but it's the celebrities and atmosphere that draw the crowds to this Covent Garden basement.

✉ 13 Exeter Street, Covent Garden ☎ (020) 7836 0651 🍴 Daily lunch, dinner 🚇 Covent Garden

Lanes (££–£££)

This elegant but friendly dining room offers a Modern European menu which is French-Italian based with a refreshing New World edge.

✉ East India House, 109–117 Middlesex Street ☎ (020) 7247 5050 🍴 Mon–Fri lunch and dinner 🚇 Liverpool Street

Lemonia (£–££)

You won't find plate-smashing at this stylish ever-popular Greek Cypriot establishment. Their set lunch is a bargain.

✉ 89 Regent's Park Road ☎ (020) 7586 7454 🍴 Mon–Fri and Sun lunch, Mon–Sat dinner 🚇 Chalk Farm

Lindsay House (£££)

Ring the bell for admission to this quirky Soho success story and succumb to the twin temptations of cutting edge cooking and sheer indulgence. Sensational, innovative, pricey dishes.

✉ 21 Romilly Street ☎ (020) 7439 0450 🍴 Mon–Fri lunch, Mon–Sat dinner 🚇 Leicester Square

Livebait (££)

Lively, informal seafood restaurant where the décor is simple and the standard of cooking and service is high.

✉ 43 The Cut ☎ (020) 7928 7211 🍴 Mon–Sat 12–11, Sun 12.30–9 🚇 Waterloo

Masala Zone (£)

Refectory type dining with an easy to negotiate menu providing a top value taste of pan-Indian cooking.

✉ 9 Marshall Street ☎ (020) 7287 9966 🍴 Daily lunch, dinner 🚇 Oxford Circus

Matsuri (£££)

The ancient art of sushi meets the modern theatrics of *teppenyaki* in this bright, festively decorated establishment.

✉ 15 Bury Street ☎ (020) 7839 1101 🍴 Mon–Sat lunch, dinner 🚇 Green Park, Piccadilly Circus

Medcalf (£)

Medcalf serves the best of Modern British cooking into the early evening and is a popular bar later on. The cooking features classic British dishes drawing from seasonal and often organic ingredients.

✉ 40 Exmouth Market ☎ (020) 7833 3533 🍴 Mon–Thu 10–8.45, Fri 10–7.45, Sun 12–5

Moro (£££)

One of the London restaurant scene's biggest recent success stories. Moro majors in the Moorish cuisine of Spain and North Africa in minimalist surroundings.

✉ **34–6 Exmouth Market**
☎ **(020) 7833 8336** Ⓓ
Mon–Fri lunch, dinner, Sat dinner only Ⓤ **Farringdon**

Navarro's (£)

Some of London's best *tapas* as well as a short menu of full traditional Spanish meals, served in an attractive tiled dining room.

✉ **67 Charlotte Street**
☎ **(020) 7637 7713** Ⓓ
Mon–Fri lunch, Mon–Sat dinner
Ⓤ **Goodge Street**

Nobu (£££)

A fun place to be—and eat in, with plenty of trendies or celebreties to look out for. Sushi and sashimi and more adventurous dishes combining Japanese and Peruvian cuisine. Book well in advance.

✉ **Metropolitan Hotel, 19 Old Park Lane** ☎ **(020) 7447 4747**
Ⓓ **Daily lunch and dinner** Ⓤ
Hyde Park Corner

Novelli in the City (££–£££)

Expect sophisticated Modern European fare from multi-Michelin starred celebrity chef Jean-Christophe Novelli in his latest restaurant housed in this private members club in the heart of the city.

✉ **London Capital Club, 15 Abchurch Lane** ☎ **(020) 7717 0088** Ⓓ **Mon–Fri 5.30–9.30 (members only for breakfast and lunch)** Ⓤ **Cannon Street, Monument, Bank**

The Oak (£–££)

This popular good value gastropub specializes in pizzas from a traditional wood-fired oven. The menu stretches to other Italian favourites and there's a good wine list too. No bookings are taken.

✉ **137 Westbourne Park Road**
☎ **(020) 7221 3355** Ⓓ
Tue–Sun lunch, dinner, Mon dinner Ⓤ **Westbourne Park**

Odette's (£££)

Very popular Modern European bistro restaurant with a lower level airy, bright conservatory and an abundance of large gilded mirrors, which give an illusion of space. It's expensive but worth the trip out to the park.

✉ **130 Regent's Park Road**
☎ **(020) 7586 5486** Ⓓ **Daily lunch, Mon–Sat dinner** Ⓤ
Chalk Farm

Quaglino's (£££)

The dining room here seats 267 and resembles an ocean liner but there's nearly always a real buzz to this theatrical restaurant. Modern European cuisine in a very French bistro/brasserie atmosphere.

✉ **16 Bury Street** ☎ **(020) 7930 6767** Ⓓ **Daily lunch, dinner** Ⓤ **Green Park**

Rasa W1 (£–££)

This restaurant's simple dining rooms on two floors feature marble floor tiles, aubergine-coloured walls and a spiral staircase between the two. The highly acclaimed vegetarian menu comes from Kerala in southern India, though meat eaters are also accommodated.

✉ **6 Dering Street** ☎ **(020) 7629 1346** Ⓓ **Mon–Sat lunch, dinner daily** Ⓤ **Bond Street**

Racine (££)

It doesn't get much more Gallic in London than this popular Knightsbridge brasserie just opposite the South Kensington museums. There's an authentic bustle and a rather masculine interior of dark wood and deep brown leather. Expect hearty bourgeois fare with big flavours.

✉ **239 Brompton Road**
☎ **(020) 7584 4477** Ⓓ
Mon–Sat lunch and dinner, Sun lunch Ⓤ **South Kensington**

Themes and Gimmicks

The Hard Rock Café started it all in 1971, Planet Hollywood (at the Trocadero) followed, while near by on Shaftesbury Avenue is the jungle of the Rainforest Café. Off-the-wall oddities include Garlic & Shots (Frith Street, Soho), a Swedish concept whereby everything (yes, everything) comes with garlic; Sarastro—The Show after the Show, Drury Lane, Covent Garden, which may appeal to operatic luvvies; and best/worst of all, the Elvis Graceland Palace on the Old Kent Road (☎ (020) 7639 3961), a little way out of the centre, but a real experience!

Pie and Mash

The nearest London comes to indigenous restaurants is the famed Pie and Mash shops. The filling in the pie used to be eels, but nowadays these are only served stewed or in aspic as jellied eels. The standard pie filling is now minced beef and the meal comes with a green sauce or gravy known as 'liquor', made from parsley. Sadly, only a few shops remain, including: Clark's, 46 Exmouth Market (☎ (020) 7837 1974; Cockneys Pie & Mash, 314 Portobello Road (☎ (020) 8960 9409; M Manze's, 87 Tower Bridge Road (☎ (020) 7407 2985)

The Ritz (£££)

A byword for style and elegance, the cooking may not quite match the fabulous setting and service. Opt for the set lunch to limit the damage to your wallet.

✉ 150 Piccadilly ☎ (020) 7493 8181 🕐 Daily lunch, dinner 🚇 Green Park

Rock and Sole Plaice (£)

A visit to this long-established fish-and-chip shop-cum-restaurant makes a good interlude, or finale, to a night of drinking in Covent Garden.

✉ 47 Endell Street ☎ (020) 7836 3785 🕐 11.30am–11pm (10pm Sun) 🚇 Covent Garden

Rules (£££)

London's oldest restaurant celebrated 200 years trading in 1998 (here Dickens dined and Edward VII and Lillie Langtry held lovers' trysts) and still draws plaudits for its top-quality British food.

✉ 34 Maiden Lane, Covent Garden ☎ (020) 7836 5314 🕐 Daily lunch, dinner 🚇 Covent Garden, Charing Cross

Soho Spice (£)

One of London's more popular Indian restaurants, relaunched in 2004 with a contemporary style of dining, featuring some unusual and tasty Anglo-Indian dishes on a short, interesting menu.

✉ 124–26 Wardour Street ☎ (020) 7434 0808 🕐 Daily lunch, dinner 🚇 Leicester Square, Tottenham Court Road

Sweetings (££)

A time-warp tourist attraction in its own right, Sweetings (established here in 1906) is one of London's oldest fish and oyster restaurants.

✉ 39 Queen Victoria Street, The City ☎ (020) 7248 3062 (no bookings) 🕐 Mon–Fri lunch 🚇 Cannon Street

Veronica's (££)

The fascinating award-winning menu here is a history lesson in British cooking with replication or adaptations of recipes going back 600 years.

✉ 3 Hereford Road ☎ (020) 7229 5079 🕐 Sun lunch, daily dinner 🚇 Bayswater, Queensway

Wagamama (£)

Located near the British Museum, this is the original Wagamama that now has five branches throughout the city. Food is eaten refectory style; a popular choice for families and vegetarians.

✉ 4a Streatham Street ☎ (020) 7323 9223 🕐 Daily lunch, dinner 🚇 Tottenham Court Road

The Wolseley (£–££)

Winner of the AA London Restaurant of the Year 2005, The Wolseley is housed in a opulent art deco building. First class Modern British café-style food is served throughout the day, perfect for breakfast or afternoon tea.

✉ 160 Piccadilly ☎ (020) 7499 6996 🕐 Mon–Fri 7am–midnight, Sat 9am–midnight, Sun 9am–11pm 🚇 Green Park

Zafferano (£££)

One of central London's best Italian restaurants. Often full of celebrities but remains unpretentious with the cooking being the focus.

✉ 15 Lowndes Street ☎ (020) 7235 5800 🕐 Daily lunch, dinner 🚇 Knightsbridge

Pubs & Wine Bars

Cork and Bottle

Typical old-fashioned London basement wine-bar, very popular after work and early evening so go later to avoid the crush.

✉ 44–46 Cranbourne Street ☎ (020) 7734 7807 🕔 Daily 🚇 Leicester Square

The Eagle

An award-winning crowd-puller, popular with media types. Serves probably the best pub food (mostly Mediterranean) in London.

✉ 159 Farringdon Road ☎ (020) 7837 1353 🕔 Mon–Sat 12–11, Sun 12–5 🚇 Farringdon

French House

This unusual pub has been a Soho institution for over 80 years. One for Francophiles, gourmets and wine-lovers, this is no place for beer drinkers but there is an excellent restaurant upstairs.

✉ 49 Dean Street ☎ (020) 7437 2799 🕔 Daily 12–11 (Sun 10:30) 🚇 Leicester Square

George Inn

London's only remaining galleried inn is a survivor from 1677, and during the summer Shakespeare's plays are performed in the courtyard. Owned by the National Trust.

✉ George Inn Yard ☎ (020) 7407 2056 🕔 Daily 🚇 London Bridge

The Holly Bush

Hidden away in a corner of old Hampstead, this simple, Edwardian wood-panelled pub is a favourite retreat when city crowds get too oppressive.

✉ 22 Holly Mount, off Heath Street, Hampstead ☎ (020) 7435 2892 🕔 Daily 🚇 Hampstead

Jerusalem Tavern

Named after the Priory of St. John in Jerusalem, this pub lies in an atmospheric corner of London. Dimly-lit bar with bare boards and rustic wooden tables. Good beer and simple bar food including speciality sandwiches and sausage baguettes.

✉ 55 Britton Street ☎ (020) 7490 4281 🕔 Mon–Fri and Sat evening 🚇 Farringdon

Lamb and Flag

Covent Garden's most characterful and atmospheric historic pub, tucked away in a small alleyway.

✉ 33 Rose Street ☎ (020) 7497 9504 🕔 Mon–Sat 11–11, Sun 12–10.30 🚇 Leicester Square, Covent Garden

The Lamb

Splendid 18th-century pub with much of its original bar woodwork and glass, including rare swivel glass 'snob screens'.

✉ Lamb's Conduit Street ☎ (020) 7405 0713 🕔 Daily 🚇 Russell Square

Prospect of Whitby

London's quintessential river pub, built in 1520, was patronised by Dickens, Turner and Whistler.

✉ 57 Wapping Wall ☎ (020) 7481 1095 🕔 Daily 🚇 Wapping

Ye Olde Cheshire Cheese

Essentially unchanged since 1667, the Cheshire Cheese is one of London's oldest and certainly most atmospheric pubs. Try their famous steak and kidney pudding.

✉ Wine Office Court, 145 Fleet Street ☎ (020) 7353 6170 🕔 Closed Sun eve 🚇 Chancery Lane, Blackfriars

Meals with a View

If you want to look down on London from your dining table the best place is the eighth-storey Oxo Tower Restaurant (► 63). There are more riverside views from Butler's Wharf Chop House (► 92), the People's Palace in the Royal Festival Hall on the South Bank and the Blueprint Café at the Design Museum (► 39). For a different perspective, ascend to the Fifth Floor Café at Harvey Nichol's (► 107), zoom up 28 floors to The Windows, at the Hilton Hotel on Park Lane or rise 24 floors up Tower 42 to Rhodes 24.

Outer London & Beyond

Outer London

Greenwich
Greenwich Union (£)
Formerly the Observatory Bar and now owned by a mirco-brewery featuring some good beers, this pub is decorated in modern style. Try the sirloin steak sandwich with caramelised onions or the good chilli con carne with soured cream or king prawns in filo pastry.
✉ 56 Royal Hill ☎ (020) 8692 6258 ⏰ Daily lunch 12–2, Mon–Sat dinner 6.30–9 🚇 DLR Greenwich 🚆 Greenwich from London Bridge

Pavilion Tea House (£)
Sitting next to the Royal Observatory on a steep hill, this splendid little park pavilion is a bright and cheerful place for fresh soups, salads, light meals, good old-fashioned English puddings and afternoon teas.
✉ Blackheath Gate, Greenwich Park ☎ (020) 8858 9695 ⏰ Daily 9–6 (closes 7 Sat, Sun) 🚤 Riverboat to Greenwich Pier 🚇 DLR Greenwich 🚆 Greenwich from London Bridge

Hampton Court
Monsieur Max (£–££)
Renowned for its excellent *cuisine bourgeoisie* served in classy surroundings.
✉ 133 High Street, Hampton Hill ☎ (020) 8979 5546 ⏰ Dinner daily, lunch Sun–Fri 🚆 Kew Gardens then 🚌 68

Kew
The Glasshouse (££–£££)
Glass fronted in keeping with its name, this smart restaurant with its sleek decor and bold modern art has a light, airy appeal. Cooking has a European slant on some traditional British favourites. Mouth-watering chocolate desserts.
✉ 14 Station Road ☎ (020) 8940 6777 ⏰ Daily lunch, dinner 🚆 Kew Gardens

The Original Maids of Honour (£)
One of London's most famous tea rooms, renowned for its delicious Maids of Honour cakes whose recipe is a closely guarded secret. Light meals.
✉ 288 Kew Road (opposite Cumberland Gate, Kew Gardens) ☎ (020) 8940 2752 ⏰ Mon 9–1, Tue–Sat 9.30–6 (lunch 12.30–2.30). Closed Sun 🚆 Kew Gardens

Richmond
Chez Lindsay (££)
Breton seafood and pancakes are the specialties of this cozy French bistro-restaurant.
✉ 11 Hill Rise ☎ (020) 8948 7473 ⏰ Daily lunch, dinner 🚆 Richmond

Outside London

Bath
The Hole in the Wall (££)
This famous, long-established cosy basement restaurant was pivotal in the development of new British cuisine.
✉ 16 George Street ☎ (01225) 425242 ⏰ Mon–Sat 12–2, 6–10

Moon and Sixpence (£)
Set in the old main post office serving excellent-value lunches and dinners. Conservatory and courtyard for summer dining.
✉ 6A Broad Street ☎ (01225) 460962 ⏰ Daily, 12–2.15, 5.30–10.45 (Sun 6.30–10.15)

The Pump Room (£–££)

Built in 1795, the decadently grand Pump Room was once the social heart of the spa city and is still an enormously popular place. Here you can taste the spa water and take the traditional lunch or tea.

✉ Stall Street (part of the Roman Baths complex)
☎ (01225) 444477 🕐 Daily 9.30–4

Sally Lunn's (£)

Savour the atmosphere of Bath's oldest house, built in 1482, while tucking into the famous (brioche-like) Bath Bun. Full meals also served.

✉ 4 North Parade Passage
☎ (01225) 461634
🕐 Mon–Sat 10am–10pm, Sun 11–10

Cambridge

Free Press (£)

In a back street not far from the city centre, this traditional town pub was named after a local 19th-century pro-temperance journal. Now serves interesting food and good real ale.

✉ Prospect Row ☎ (01223) 368337 🕐 Mon–Fri 12–2.30, 6–11, Sat 12–3, 6–11, Sun 12–3, 7–10.30

Midsummer House (£££)

Victorian villa on the Riverside serving modern French-Mediterranean fare.

✉ Midsummer Common
☎ (01223) 369299 🕐 Tue–Sat 12–2, 7–10

Oxford

Brown's (£)

Buzzing, informal restaurant with a wide range of popular classic brasserie dishes at reasonable prices.

✉ 5 Woodstock Road
☎ (01865) 511995 🕐 Mon–Sat 11am–11.30pm, Sun 12–11 (last orders 9)

Nosebag (£)

Homemade quiches, salads, soups and sandwiches plus imaginative daily special dishes have students and visitors queuing at this attractive restaurant.

✉ 6 St. Michael's Street
☎ (01865) 721033 🕐 Daily from 9.30am; closes Mon 5.30, Tue–Thu 10pm, Fri–Sat 10.30pm, Sun 9pm

Le Petit Blanc (££)

Owned by culinary maestro Raymond Blanc, but with prices that won't make grown men weep, this is a splendid taste of Modern European cooking in a stylish, cosmopolitan, town centre brasserie.

✉ 71–72 Walton Street
☎ (01865) 510999
🕐 Daily lunch, dinner

Windsor

Aurora Garden Hotel (£–££)

The conservatory restaurant in this pleasant hotel is a relaxing setting for a meal, with lovely evening views of the water gardens. The menu has classic dishes such as loin of lamb with redcurrant jus.

✉ Bolton Avenue ☎ (01753) 868686 🕐 Daily 12–2, 7–7.30. Closed Sat lunch

The Castle Hotel (£££)

In the regal shadow of Windsor's great castle, the popular and inventive restaurant combines traditional themes with modern culinary ideas.

✉ High Street, Windsor
☎ 0870 400 8300 🕐 Tue–Sun dinner, Sun lunch only

Gilbey's Bar and Restaurant (£)

Book a conservatory table at this popular restaurant just over the footbridge spanning the Thames, dividing Windsor and Eton. Good inventive menu and very reasonable wine prices.

✉ High Street, Eton
☎ (01753) 854921 🕐 Daily 12–2.30/3, 6–10.30 (Sat 11)

Cream Tea

Try to take an early lunch when making an excursion out of London in order to leave time and space for that most English of institutions, the cream tea. Not so fussy or substantial as formal afternoon tea (► 61) a traditional cream tea comprises a pot of tea with two scones, cream and strawberry jam. It's often too much for one person so you may want to share the scones.

Central London

Hotel Prices

All prices are for one night's double room, whatever the occupancy – though American visitors should note that it is rare for a whole family to be allowed to share.

£ = up to £100
££ = £100–£200
£££ = over £200

Athenaeum (£££)

This elegant hotel overlooking Green Park remains one of the most popular and friendly in the area. Lovely bedrooms and a spa for the exclusive use of guests.

✉ Piccadilly ☎ (020) 7499 3464; www.athenaeum.com
Ⓖ Green Park

Avonmore Hotel (£–££)

A privately owned AA award-winning B&B with just nine bedrooms and a friendly atmosphere.

✉ 66 Avonmore Road, Kensington ☎ (020) 7603 3121; www.avonmorehotel.co.uk
Ⓖ West Kensington

Basil Street (£££)

A traditional and friendly hotel in the heart of Knightsbridge. The public rooms are full of character with antiques, parquet floors, fine paintings and tapestries.

✉ Basil Street ☎ (020) 7581 3311; www.thebasil.com
Ⓖ Knightsbridge

Beaufort (££)

This small award-winning hotel, situated in a quiet tree-lined square near Harrods, is comfortably furnished with lots of individual extras.

✉ 33 Beaufort Gardens ☎ (020) 7584 5252; www.thebeaufort.co.uk
Ⓖ Knightsbridge

The Berkeley (£££)

This traditional hotel, with views over Hyde Park, offers exemplary standards of accommodation and service. It has beautiful rooms and first-class leisure facilities.

✉ Wilton Place, Knightsbridge ☎ (020) 7950 5490; www.savoygroup.co.uk
Ⓖ Knightsbridge

Byron (££)

A charming terraced house, thoughtfully restored. Bedrooms are comfortable and tastefully furnished.

✉ 36–38 Queensborough Terrace ☎ (020) 7243 0987; www.capricornhotels.co.uk
Ⓖ Queensway

Capital (£££)

Small and exclusive, the Capital, set in the heart of Knightsbridge, attracts a loyal clientele. Superb restaurant (► 93).

✉ Basil Street ☎ (020) 7589 5171; www.capitalhotel.co.uk
Ⓖ Knightsbridge

Claridge's (£££)

A London institution welcoming royalty and heads of state for almost a century. Supremely comfortable bedrooms and opulent public areas.

✉ Brook Street ☎ (020) 7629 8860; www.claridgeshotel.com
Ⓖ Bond Street

Comfort Inn, Vauxhall (£)

Recently built and in a good location to access central London. The spacious bedrooms are modern and comfortable. Cafeteria-style breakfast.

✉ 87 South Lambeth Road ☎ (020) 7735 9494; www.comfortinnvx.co.uk
Ⓖ Vauxhall

The Connaught (£££)

Perhaps the most discreet and reserved of London's great hotels, retaining its century-old atmosphere. One of London's best restaurant's is here (► 93).

✉ Carlos Place ☎ (020) 7499 7070; www.savoygroup.co.uk
Ⓖ Bond Street

County Hall Premier Travel Inn Metro (£)

The most economical, central base for a family stay in London, right below the London Eye (➤ 33), cheek by jowl with London Aquarium (➤ 51) and a stroll across the bridge from Big Ben.

✉ **Belvedere Road** ☎ **0870 238 3300; www.travelinn.co.uk** 🚇 **Waterloo, Westminster**

Delmere (£–££)

Smart friendly staff, well-equipped rooms, a jazz-themed bar and particularly comfortable lounge are the main attractions of this boutique hotel near Hyde Park.

✉ **130 Sussex Gardens** ☎ **(020) 7706 3344; www.delmerehotels.com** 🚇 **Paddington**

Dorchester (£££)

One of the world's finest hotels. Renowned for its beautifully furnished bedrooms and sumptuous bathrooms.

✉ **Park Lane** ☎ **(020) 7629 8888; www.dorchesterhotel.com** 🚇 **Hyde Park Corner**

The Goring (£££)

Among London's most famous quality small hotels, providing a wonderful example of old-fashioned hospitality and service.

✉ **Beeston Place, Grosvenor Gardens** ☎ **(020) 7396 9000; www.goringhotel.co.uk** 🚇 **Victoria**

The Halkin (£££)

One of London's most individual and attractive hotels, contemporary in design, with stylish fully air-conditioned bedrooms. Fine dining in the Thai restaurant.

✉ **Halkin Street, Belgravia** ☎ **(020) 7333 1000; www.haldin.co.uk** 🚇 **Hyde Park Corner**

Hart House Hotel (££)

This elegant Georgian town house is part of a terrace of mansions that were home to French nobility during the French Revolution. It has been lovingly restored by the owner.

✉ **51 Gloucester Place, Portman Square** ☎ **(020) 7935 2288; www.harthouse.co.uk** 🚇 **Baker Street**

Hilton Waldorf (£££)

The Waldorf goes from strength to strength with a recent injection of enthusiastic and committed managerial staff. The Palm Court Lounge is a London legend.

✉ **Aldwych** ☎ **(020) 7836 2400; www.hilton.co.uk** 🚇 **Charing Cross**

Ibis Euston (£)

Bright, well-maintained bedrooms, a public bar-lounge and a secure covered car park make this popular hotel good value for its central location, near Euston station.

✉ **3 Cardington Street** ☎ **(020) 7388 7777; www.ibishotel.com** 🚇 **Euston**

The Lanesborough (£££)

Famous London landmark on Hyde Park Corner with superbly appointed, thoughtfully equipped bedrooms, and butlers to offer the highest standards of personal service.

✉ **Hyde Park Corner** ☎ **(020) 7259 5599; www.lanesborough.com** 🚇 **Hyde Park Corner**

Hotel Ratings

Most hotel rates are inclusive of all taxes, service charges and breakfast, which usually means full English breakfast (➤ 61), though do check this. Perversely, only the most expensive hotels have the temerity to charge extra for breakfast.

On a Budget

Travellers on a wafer-thin budget should consider staying at one of London's 18 YMCA/YWCA hostels or at one of the seven YHA hostels. The YHA hostels in particular are extremely good value and in surprisingly central locations, consequently you'll generally need to book at least three months ahead for the summer. Contact the YMCA/YWCA at 640 Forest Road E17 ☎ (020) 8520 5599; www.ymca.org.uk, and the YHA, Trevelyan House, Dimple Road, Matlock, Derbyshire, DE4 3YH ☎ 0870 870 8868; reservations 0870 770 6113; fax 0870 770 6127; www.yha.org.uk; e-mail: reservations@yha.org.uk.

Mandarin Oriental, Hyde Park (£££)

Once used as residential chambers for Victorian gentlemen, this traditional building has been updated with individually decorated and spacious rooms.

✉ 66 Knightsbridge ☎ (020) 7235 2000; www.mandarin oriental.com 🚇 Knightsbridge

Le Meridien Piccadilly (£££)

For many, this well-established luxury hotel lies at the very hub of London life. Bedrooms are finished to a high standard.

✉ 21 Piccadilly ☎ 0870 400 8400; www.lemeridien.com 🚇 Piccadilly Circus

Mitre House Hotel (£)

Housed in a Grade II listed building, this is a long-established family-run hotel with 70 rooms and offering good facilities. Close to Hyde Park.

✉ 178–84 Sussex Gardens ☎ (020) 7723 8040; www.mitrehousehotel.com 🚇 Lancaster Gate

Norfolk Plaza (£–££)

Comfortable hotel located in a quiet residential square and within easy walking distance of the West End.

✉ 29–33 Norfolk Square, Paddington ☎ (020) 7723 0792; www.norfolkplazahotel.co.uk 🚇 Paddington

One Aldwych (£££)

This former AA Hotel of the Year is perhaps the most stylish newcomer to the capital in years; the ultimate in chic minimalist luxury.

✉ 1 Aldwych ☎ (020) 7300 1000; www.onealdwych.com 🚇 Charing Cross, Covent Garden

Quality Hotel, Hampstead (££)

Friendly hotel close to Hampstead Heath; popular with overseas visitors. Bedrooms are thoughtfully equipped.

✉ 5–7 Frognal, Hampstead ☎ (020) 7835 2000; www.lth-hotels.com 🚇 Hampstead

The Ritz (£££)

A London legend with a reputation that stretches around the globe. The sumptuous bedrooms are furnished in Louis XVI style and the public rooms are palatial (► 96).

✉ 150 Piccadilly ☎ (020) 7493 8181; www.theritz london.com 🚇 Green Park

The Savoy (£££)

A London institution. High standards of comfort and quality with many of its famous features preserved, including the art deco styling.

✉ Strand ☎ (020) 7836 4343; www.thesavoygroup.co.uk 🚇 Charing Cross

The Stafford (£££)

Tucked away in exclusive St. James, offering the height of luxury. Elegant, individually designed bedrooms and beautiful public areas.

✉ 16–18 St. James's Place ☎ (020) 7493 0111; www.the staffordhotel.co.uk 🚇 Green Park

Swiss House Hotel (£)

Comfortable, well-situated 16-room hotel in a pretty, residential area of South Kensington, convenient for museums and shopping.

✉ 171 Old Brompton Road ☎ (020) 7373 2769; www.swiss-hh.demon.co.uk 🚇 South Kensington

Central London & Excursions

Thistle Tower (££)

Large, busy, modern hotel next to the Tower of London with views of Tower Bridge and St. Katharine's Dock.

✉ **St. Katharine's Way**
☎ **0870 333 9106;**
www.thistlehotels.com
Ⓣ **Tower Hill**

Travelodge (£)

Located in a quiet spot not far from Liverpool Street station; adequate rooms at a good rate. Ideal for families.

✉ **1 Harrow Lodge** ☎ **(020) 0870 191 1689;**
www.travelodge.co.uk
Ⓣ **Liverpool Street**

Wigmore Court(££)

Conveniently positioned with bright and welcoming public areas and equally appealing bedrooms.

✉ **23 Gloucester Place**
☎ **(020) 7935 0928;**
www.wigmore-court-hotel.co.uk Ⓣ **Baker Street**

Outside London

Bath

Bath Tasburgh (£–££)

Set in beautifully tended grounds, this charming Victorian House has views over the Avon Valley. The adjacent canal towpath provides a walk into town.

✉ **Warminster Road**
☎ **(01225) 425096;**
www.bathtasburgh.co.uk

Haringtons (££)

Located in a picturesque cobbled city-centre street, this friendly hotel offers a high standard of modern comforts within a distinctive 18th-century building.

✉ **8–10 Queen Street**
☎ **(01225) 461728;**
www.hartingtons.co.uk

Cambridge

Arundel House (£–££)

The Arundel looks out onto the river and open parkland. Ask for the bedrooms in the converted coach house.

✉ **Chesterton Road**
☎ **(01223) 367701;**
www.arundelhousehotels.co.uk

Oxford

The Macdonald Randolph (££)

This famous landmark hotel in the centre of Oxford has a timeless elegance and many superb architectural features.

✉ **Beaumont Street** ☎ **0870 830 4817; www.randolph-hotel.com**

The Macdonald Eastgate (££)

A relaxing English country house hotel, ideally situated at the heart of the historic town close to the Thames and Magdalen Bridge.

✉ **The High, at the corner of Merton Street** ☎ **0870 400 8201;**
www.macdonaldhotels.co.uk

Windsor

Aurora Garden (£–££)

Small, friendly hotel set in a residential area a few minutes' stroll from the town. The food is very good and diners look out onto a landscaped water garden (► 99).

✉ **Bolton Avenue** ☎ **(01753) 868686;**
www.auroragarden.co.uk

Ye Harte and Garter (£–££)

This hotel enjoys views of Windsor Castle, offers high standards of accommodation and a taste of Olde England.

✉ **High Street** ☎ **(01753) 863426;**
www.harteandgarter.com

Booking a Bed

If you arrive in London without accommodation, don't worry. You can make same-day bookings at the the Visitor Centre, 1 Regent Street. There is a small charge for this service.

Useful websites

www.londonhomestay.co.uk
www.londonnet.co.uk

Shopping Areas

Shop Opening Times

Traditionally London shop opening hours have been Monday to Saturday 9.30–6. Many West End stores stay open later on Thursdays; in Knightsbridge late night is Wednesdays. More recently, however, several shops are opening later at other times and also on Sunday (from 11 or 12). If opening times are not indicated in the entry then you can assume that they operate more-or-less traditional hours. In tourist enclaves such as Covent Garden, Sunday opening is the norm.

Bond Street

London's most exclusive shopping street is expensive for buying, but a great place for just looking. *Haute couture*, antiques, auction houses, fine-art galleries and jewellers predominate.

🚇 **Green Park, Bond Street**

Charing Cross Road

A bookworm's heaven, for both new and used books. For general browsing try Blackwells, Books Etc, Foyles (► 105) or Waterstone's. For specialist, second-hand and antiquarian books go to Cecil Court, off Charing Cross Road.

🚇 **Leicester Square, Tottenham Court Road**

Covent Garden–Neal Street

Specialization is the key here with The Kite Store, The Tea House, The Astrology Shop, and many other one-off stars. Neal's Yard attracts wholefood lovers, while young shoppers come for the high fashion on Short's Gardens.

🚇 **Covent Garden**

Covent Garden Piazza

Lots of small, individual, often idiosyncratic, shops in a buzzing traffic-free environment.

🚇 **Covent Garden**

Jermyn Street

Both a historical attraction and a shopping street, Jermyn Street is London shopping at its old-fashioned best. (► 48)

🚇 **Green Park,**

Kensington

Cheap and retro clothing can be found at Kensington Market, antiques and art abound on up-market Kensington Church Street, and behind the beautiful art deco front of Barkers is a smart arcade.

🚇 **Kensington High Street**

King's Road

Birthplace of the mini-skirt and the Punk movement, the King's Road is still up-to-the-minute on street fashion, but is less radical these days. This is also a good place to buy antiques and curios.

🚇 **Sloane Square**

Oxford Street

London's most frenetic shopping street presents a cacophony of global styles and noise and is generally only worth patronising for its department stores. However, off here at St. Christopher's Place and South Molton Street (immediately north and south of Bond Street tube respectively) are some cutting-edge designer-fashion outlets.

🚇 **Marble Arch, Bond Street, Oxford Circus, Tottenham Court Rd**

Regent Street

A handsome boulevard with many exclusive shops including gold, silver and jewellery at Mappin & Webb and Garrard & Co; toys at Hamley's (► 111), and all sorts at Liberty (► 107).

🚇 **Oxford Circus**

Sloane Street

Armani, Chanel, Dior, Gucci, D&G, Hermès, Katharine Hamnett, Tommy Hilfiger and Valentino are just some of the designer names to be found here.

🚇 **Sloane Square (south end), Knightsbridge (north end)**

Antiques & Books

Antiques

Alfie's Antique Market

Alfie's is a London institution. Don't miss the post-war kitchenware in the basement!

✉ 13–25 Church Street
☎ (020) 7723 6066
Ⓜ Edgware Road, Marylebone Road

Antiquarius

This attractive fashionable Chelsea arcade holds around 100 dealers covering a wide range of wares.

✉ 131–41 King's Road
☎ (020) 7351 5353
🕐 Mon–Sat 10–6 Ⓜ Sloane Square then 🚌 11, 19 or 22

Bermondsey (New Caledonian) Market

London's prime market for serious antiques collectors and the trade, who snap up most of the bargains shortly after the horribly early opening hour of 5am.

✉ Bermondsey Square
🕐 Fri 5am–2pm (starts closing at 12) Ⓜ London Bridge

Camden Passage

Located not in Camden, but in trendy Islington, with one of the biggest concentrations of antiques in the whole country. Dozens of high-quality dealers but few bargains.

✉ Off Upper Street 🕐 Wed 10–2, Sat 10–5 Ⓜ Angel

Chelsea Antiques Market

Claimed to be the oldest antiques market in Britain, the dealers here cover most interests and at prices that are relatively good value compared to the Kings Road.

✉ 245a–253 King's Road
☎ (020) 7352 5689 Ⓜ Sloane Square

Portobello Road

(Markets, ► 108–109)

Books

Any Amount of Books

You'll find thousands of second-hand general-interest volumes here, and they are well ordered so that browsing is a pleasure instead of a chore.

✉ 62 Charing Cross Road
☎ (020) 7836 3697
Ⓜ Leicester Square

Forbidden Planet

The extraterrestrial monsters in the window tell you what to expect at this sci-fi/fantasy mecca. Videos, toys, comics and magazines too. A good place to take the kids.

✉ 179 Shaftesbury Avenue
☎ (020) 7420 3666
Ⓜ Tottenham Court Road

Foyles

Despite its apparent disorder, this is the biggest book shop in Britain so you're sure to find what you want here—eventually.

✉ 113–119 Charing Cross Road
☎ (020) 7437 5660
Ⓜ Tottenham Court Rd

Stanford's

The world's largest travel book shop with a vast selection of guides, travelogues and maps to everywhere on earth.

✉ 12–14 Long Acre ☎ (020) 7836 1321 Ⓜ Leicester Square

Waterstone's

Probably the best alternative to Foyles (► above) for that elusive volume. Good second-hand department.

✉ 82 Gower Street ☎ (020) 7636 1577 🕐 Daily
Ⓜ Tottenham Court Road

Presents from the Past

Some of the best high-quality individual souvenirs and gifts are to be found in museum shops. You don't have to pay to get in as they are outside the turnstiles, or you will be issued with a special (free) ticket. The British Museum, the South Kensington museums and the Design Museum are particularly noteworthy, while The Museum Store at 37 The Market, Covent Garden Piazza, goes a step further, trawling the best of the world's museums for ideas.

Clothing, Cosmetics & Department Stores

London's Arcades

American cities have shopping malls, London has arcades. These covered walkways full of small individual shops, many of which are jewellers and antiques dealers, provide a fascinating glimpse into the past. The best example is Burlington Arcade (off Piccadilly), built in 1819, where beadles in top hats and great coats still ensure that decorum is maintained. Directly opposite, running down to Jermyn Street, is Piccadilly Arcade and just around the corner, connecting Old Bond Street to Albemarle Street, is Royal Arcade. Also off Jermyn Street is Princes Arcade.

Clothing and Accessories

Bates the Hatter

London's favourite hat shop has been topping off the famous (and not-so-famous) since 1902 in panamas, trilbys, top hats and the like.
✉ **21a Jermyn Street** ☎ **(020) 7734 2722** 🚇 **Piccadilly Circus**

Brown's

One of London's best designer boutiques claiming to hold the biggest range of labels. For discount gear try their branch Brown's Labels for Less, just a few yards away at 50 South Molton Street.
✉ **23–27 South Molton Street** ☎ **(020) 7514 0000** 🚇 **Bond Street**

Burberry's

The famous Burberry check is not just confined to trenchcoats and scarves. Choose from over 300 lines at this very British institution.
✉ **18–22 Haymarket** ☎ **(020) 7930 3343** 🚇 **Piccadilly Circus**

Fenwick

If you're in Bond Street but don't want to go in the designer boutiques, this unintimidating department store carries many of the same names.
✉ **63 New Bond Street** ☎ **(020) 7629 9161** 🚇 **Bond Street**

Laura Ashley

Typecast as the quintessential English rose, Laura Ashley has been revamped to include more daring modern fashions..
✉ **256–258 Regent Street** ☎ **(020) 7437 9760** 🚇 **Oxford Circus**

Lillywhite's

The last name in branded sports clothing, with traditional British sports best represented, though you will find there is stock from all over the world.
✉ **24–36 Lower Regent Street** ☎ **0870 333 9600** 🚇 **Piccadilly Circus**

Paul Smith

One of Britain's most successful designers, Paul Smith takes classics and adds a twist or two. Large range at this branch—try the big department stores, too.
✉ **40–44 Floral Street** ☎ **(020) 7379 7133** 🚇 **Covent Garden**

Turnbull & Asser

Off the peg and made to measure shirts for men in true classic British design. This is the haunt of royalty and traditonalists.
✉ **71–72 Jermyn Street** ☎ **(020) 7808 3000** 🚇 **Green Park, Piccadilly Circus**

Urban Outfitters

Supplies the trend-concious young with the latest in streetwear and the newest accessories. Constantly updating and supplying new fashion labels.
✉ **36–38 Kensington High Street** ☎ **(020) 7761 1001** 🚇 **High Street Kensington**

Beauty & Cosmetics

Floris

Elegant and very classy, London's oldest perfumery was established in 1730 and is a tourist attraction in its own right.
✉ **89 Jermyn Street** ☎ **(020) 7930 2885** 🚇 **Green Park**

Jo Malone

Lovely shop selling all kinds of perfume, face creams and great gifts including gorgeous scented candles. Jo Malone is internationally acclaimed for her facials using her own products.

✉ **150 Sloane Street** ☎ **(020) 7720 0202** Ⓟ **Sloane Square**

Molton Brown

A seductive aroma greets you as you cross the threshold. Shampoos, bath oils and scented candles that are hard to resist.

✉ **58 Molton Street** ☎ **(020) 7499 6474** Ⓟ **Bond Street**

Neal's Yard Remedies

Delicious-smelling, stylish, Covent Garden herbalist, selling essential oils and homeopathic remedies of all kinds.

✉ **15 Neal's Yard** ☎ **(020) 7379 7222** Ⓟ **Covent Garden**

Penhaligon's

Beautiful Victorian shopfront and fittings with colognes and powders, perfumes and accessories. Several branches.

✉ **41 Wellington Street** ☎ **(020) 7836 2150** Ⓟ **Covent Garden**

Department Stores

Fortnum & Mason

Predating the supermarket, the Fortnum & Mason's Food Hall has been supplying the nobility with parcels and hampers since the days of Queen Victoria and is the main attraction at this classy department store.

✉ **Piccadilly** ☎ **(020) 7734 8040** Ⓟ **Piccadilly Circus, Green Park**

Harrods

London's ultimate shopping experience (➤ 44).

✉ **Knightsbridge** ☎ **(020) 7730 1234** Ⓟ **Knightsbridge**

❓ **Dress code: no scruffy attire, very short or cylcing shorts**

Harvey Nichols

Worth looking at for its renowned window displays 'Harvey Nicks' is the favourite shop of London's rich young things but also has a surprisingly good menswear department and a mouth-watering food hall.

✉ **67 Brompton Road** ☎ **(020) 7235 5000** Ⓟ **Knightsbridge**

Liberty

Famously associated with the art nouveau and developing design oriented printed fabrics, the interior of London's most beautiful store comprises series of four-storey galleries around a central well, draped with oriental carpets.

✉ **210–220 Regent Street** ☎ **(020) 7734 1234** Ⓟ **Oxford Circus**

Marks & Spencer

This is the biggest branch of one of Britain's favourite stores with consistently high quality and value across its range.

✉ **458 Oxford Street** ☎ **(020) 7935 7954** Ⓟ **Marble Arch**

Selfridges

The magnificent art deco and Ionic pillar frontage promises more than the store actually delivers. Probably best for clothes, though there's also a good food hall and a huge perfume department.

✉ **400 Oxford Street** ☎ **0870 837 7377** Ⓟ **Bond Street**

By Royal Appointment

Many of London's top shops claim a Royal Warrant of Appointment. These can only be granted by the Queen, the Queen Mother, the Prince of Wales and the Duke of Edinburgh and each signifies that one of these members of the royal family has patronised the shop for at least three years. The coat (or coats) of arms on display outside the shop indicates which member.

Furnishings, Food, Markets & Music

Shop 'til you Drop
Serious shoppers should invest in the *Time Out Guide to Shopping & Services.* Equally useful to locals and visitors, it includes well over 1,000 reviews of all that's best in the capital. Some issues feature a discount card that may return your investment with interest.

Design and Furnishings

Conran Shop
Let style guru Sir Terence Conran counsel you on household accessories, furniture and food. Worth a visit for the splendid art deco building which also houses Bibendum (➤ 92).
- 🖂 Michelin House, 81 Fulham Road ☎ (020) 7589 7401
- 🕓 Daily (Sun 12–6)
- 🚇 South Kensington

General Trading Company
This company has been going since 1920 albeit in new premises since 2001. The whole place is laid out like a stylish home stocking furniture, tableware and gifts.
- 🖂 2 Symons Street ☎ (020) 7730 0411 🚇 Sloane Square

Heal's
A wide range of furnishings and accessories that live up to the store's claim of 'style, quality and exclusivity'—but at a price.
- 🖂 196 Tottenham Court Road ☎ (020) 7636 1666 🚇 Goodge Street

Oxo Tower
Some of London's funkiest new designers show off their wares in equally stylish surroundings (➤ 63). Very expensive, but good just to look at.
- 🖂 Oxo Tower Wharf, Riverside Walk/Bargehouse Street ☎ (020) 7401 2255
- 🕓 Tue–Sun 11–6 🚇 Waterloo

Food and Drink

Berry Brothers & Rudd
One of London's most venerable and attractive shops, dating from the early 19th century, houses this quintessential traditional London wine merchant.
- 🖂 3 St. James's Street
- ☎ (020) 7396 9600
- 🚇 Green Park

Fortnum & Mason (➤ 107)

Neal's Yard Dairy
Splendid rustic-style shop selling only British and Irish cheeses in tip-top condition.
- 🖂 17 Short's Gardens
- ☎ (020) 7240 5700
- 🚇 Covent Garden

Markets

Berwick Street Market
The West End's best fruit and vegetable market is a boon to locals and self-catering visitors. Loud and lively stallholders and lots of local colour.
- 🖂 Berwick Street, Rupert Street 🕓 Mon–Sat 8–6
- 🚇 Leicester Square, Piccadilly Circus

Brick Lane
Get the real flavour of the East End with fruit and vegetables, clothes, bric-à-brac, oddities and pure junk. A great place for people-watching.
- 🖂 Brick Lane and environs
- 🕓 Sun 6am–1pm 🚇 Aldgate East, Shoreditch

Camden Lock
This is the arts and craft arm of the famous Camden Market (➤ 109), open during the week. Jewellery and clothing Saturday and Sunday. Good ethnic fast food, too.
- 🖂 Camden Lock Place, off Chalk Farm Road 🕓 Daily 10–6
- 🚇 Camden Town

Camden Market

London's most colourful street market, famous for its street fashions, jewellery and ceramics, keeps growing. The latest offerings are 20th-century collectables and an organic food market. Great atmosphere.

✉ **Camden High Street**
🕐 **Thu–Sun 9–5.30**
🚇 **Camden Town**

Covent Garden

The Jubilee Market for leather, clothes and cheap CDs Tue–Fri and crafts at weekends. The central Apple Market for arts and crafts. Antiques at both, Mondays.

✉ **Jubilee Market, The Piazza/Southampton Street; Apple Market, The Piazza**
🕐 **Both daily, 9–5** 🚇 **Covent Garden**

Greenwich

A whole host of enjoyable lively weekend markets congregate around the main market hall off Greenwich Church Street. Sunday is best, when you'll find ethnic jewellery, pottery, antiques, clothes, arts, crafts and much more.

✉ **Around Greenwich Church Street/High Road and College Approach** 🕐 **Sat–Sun 9–6**
🚇 **Greenwich mainline or DLR**

Leadenhall Market

A classic Victorian glass and iron hall, built in the 1880s, is the splendid home of the City's 600-year-old street market. Beautiful displays of fresh fish, game and poultry, meats and cheese, flowers and fruit.

✉ **Whittington Avenue, off Gracechurch Street**
🕐 **Mon–Fri 7–4**
🚇 **Monument, Bank**

Petticoat Lane

London's best-known street market attracts tourist tat but there's plenty of worthwhile stuff here too, particularly leather goods.

✉ **Middlesex Street and environs** 🕐 **Sun 9–2 (Wentworth Street also open Mon–Fri 10–2.30)** 🚇 **Liverpool Street**

Portobello Road

Around 2,000 antiques traders set up stall here every Saturday along this bustling mile-long stretch you'll find food, clothing and designer street-wear. Come on Saturday for buskers and reggae vibes.

✉ **Portobello Road and environs** 🕐 **General market Mon–Wed 9–5, Thu 9–1, Fri–Sat 7–6. Antiques Sat 6am–6pm**
🚇 **Notting Hill Gate**

Music

Virgin

The biggest of London's music megastores. Not only popular, chart stuff, but also excellent specialist, classical, jazz, folk and import stocks.

✉ **1 Piccadilly Circus (branches at Queensway, Camden High Street and Kensington High Street)**
☎ **(020) 7439 2500**
🕐 **Mon–Sat 9am–midnight, Sun 12–6** 🚇 **Piccadilly Circus**

Chappell of Bond Street

Located among some of the smartest shops in town, Chappells has the largest selection of classical and popular sheet music in the UK. Also keyboards, brass and woodwind instruments.

✉ **50 New Bond Street**
☎ **(020) 7491 2777**
🚇 **Bond Street**

Tax-free Shopping

If you hold a non-EU passport then it is worth enquiring about the tax-free shopping export scheme, which will enable you to claim back VAT (Value Added Tax) when you leave the country. This is currently rated at 17 per cent and is payable on most goods (books, food and children's clothes are the principal exceptions). All department stores and many other participating outlets (look for the TAX-FREE sticker) will give you details. Most will require a minimum purchase.

Children's Attractions

Backstage Tours
Older children and teens may enjoy the opportunity to look behind the scenes in London. See how scenery, props and costumes are made at the National Theatre (➤ 112), or take a look at the work inspired by the Bard at the Royal Shakespeare Company's Barbican and Pit theatres (➤ 112) and the elaborate Royal Opera House for ballet and opera sets (➤ 113). For sporting children there are tours of Wimbledon's All England Lawn Tennis Club (☎ (020) 8946 6131), the MCC at Lord's cricket ground (☎ (020) 7616 8595) and the Rugby Football Union Stadium at Twickenham (☎ (020) 8892 8877). Reservations are essential for all and some are very expensive.

Central London

All Creatures Great and Small
The dinosaurs at the Natural History Museum (➤ 21) and the inmates of London Zoo (➤ 55) are perennial favourites. The London Aquarium (➤ 51) is another good bet.

Brass Rubbings
While mum or dad is admiring the church of St. Martin-in-the-Fields (➤ 75) the kids can make their own historical creation by rubbing wax crayons on to a sheet of paper on ancient (and not so ancient) church brasses.

Covent Garden
You can't go wrong here with children. The pedestrianized central area has free outdoor entertainment, bright lively shops and market stalls selling children's items, and lots of informal eating choices.

Hands-on!
Many of London's major museums now have specific interactive exhibits for children. The best are at the Science Museum (➤ 23) and the National Maritime Museum (➤ 82).

History in the Making
Family favourites include the Beefeaters with their blood 'n' thunder stories of the Tower of London (➤ 24); the historical spectacle and child-friendly actors of Hampton Court Palace (➤ 85) and the spectacular hardware at the Imperial War Museum (➤ 46).

Museums
London's major children's museum is aimed as much at nostalgic adults as kids.

Bethnal Green Museum of Childhood (➤ 57)

Ship Ahoy!
Clambering aboard deck is always a popular option and the older the vessel, the more the enjoyment. London has a number of historical ships including the *Cutty Sark* (➤ 84) and HMS *Belfast* (➤ 44). River cruises are also a favourite.

Duck Tours
London's most unusual river ride is aboard a yellow amphibious ex-World War II DUKW (Duck) vehicle, operated by Duck Tours. It begins, in conventional style on dry land, but just watch the kids' faces as their land vehicle suddenly splashes into the water.
✉ Belvedere Road (behind County Hall) ☎ (020) 7928 3132 (booking essential)
🎫 Expensive

Golden Hinde
Take a look around this replica of Sir Francis Drake's flagship.
✉ Golden Hinde, St. Mary Overie Dock, beside Southwark Cathedral ⏰ Daily 10–6 ☎ 0870 0118 700 🚇 London Bridge

Thrills...

Namco Station
Next to the London Eye is London's largest interactive entertainment venue with games arcades, ten-pin bowling, bumper cars, pool and lots more for teens.

✉ County Hall ☎ (020) 7967 1066 ⏰ Daily 10–midnight
🚇 Waterloo

The Trocadero
Techno-thrills, state-of-the-art motion-simulator rides and virtual reality adventures await here. Expect long queues.
✉ Piccadilly Circus ☎ (020) 7439 1791 ⏰ Daily 10–10
🚇 Piccadilly Circus

... and Chills
The horribly realistic blood and gore of Madame Tussaud's Chamber of Horrors (➤ 56) and particularly the London Dungeon (➤ 54) are perennially popular with teenagers—but unsuitable for young children.

Restaurants
Older children and teenagers love Planet Hollywood at the Trocadero Centre, while the Hard Rock Café (➤ 95) is an evergreen. Close by, on Shaftesbury Avenue, the Rainforest Café is a jungle-themed restaurant for younger children.

Smollensky's on the Strand
Come for lunch at the weekend when the special children's entertainment includes clowns, magic shows, face painting and PS2 games. Live jazz, Latin and soul music every Sunday.
✉ 105 Strand ☎ (020) 7497 2101 🚇 Embankment, Charing Cross

Shopping

Hamley's
The world's greatest toy shop can be horribly busy (go on a weekday in term time if possible) but the range is enormous.
✉ 188–196 Regent Street
☎ 0870 333 2450
⏰ Mon–Fri 10–8, Sat 9.30–8, Sun 12–6 🚇 Oxford Circus

Theatres

Little Angel Theatre
Puppet shows every Saturday and Sunday at 11am and 2pm (age range varies call first for details). Additional shows during school holidays.
✉ 14 Dagmar Passage, off Cross Street, Islington ☎ (020) 7226 1787 🚇 Angel, Highbury & Islington

Unicorn Theatre
Purpose designed theatre for children in London covering a range of activities including mime, puppet shows and plays. Performances are at 11.30am and 2.30pm on Sat and Sun with additional shows during school holidays.
✉ St. Mark's Studio, Chillingworth Road ☎ (020) 7697 1150 🚇 London Bridge

Outside London

Windsor
Windsor Castle (➤ 90)
Curious young children will enjoy the Doll's House.

Legoland
This gloriously landscaped theme-park in miniature, designed for the under-12s, is one of the best children's attractions in the country.
✉ Winkfield Road ⏰ Daily mid-Mar from 10am (until 7 during school hols) ☎ 0870 504 0404 ;www.legoland.co.uk 💰 Very expensive 🚌 Shuttle from Windsor town centre, by castle

Theme Parks
Just outside London are Chessington World of Adventures (☎ 0870 444 7777) and Thorpe Park (☎ 0870 444 4466). The former is more suitable for teenagers, with plenty of hairy, white-knuckle rides, while the latter is aimed at younger children, and has a number of water-rides.

Sleepovers
Fancy spending a night with a dinosaur or aboard a sailing ship? The Natural History Museum (➤ 21) and the *Golden Hinde* (➤ 110) both organize sleepovers for groups of children. Contact them for details.

Theatre

What's On?
The listings on these pages contain only the best and the most famous of London's many entertainment options—which is a tiny proportion of the total offering. For the most comprehensive listing and best reviews buy *Time Out* magazine (aimed more at Londoners) or alternatively *What's On in London* (aimed more at visitors), both available weekly from most newsagents.

The West End
Many West End theatres feature famous long-running musicals (*Cats*, *Les Misérables*, *Phantom of the Opera* and so on). Tickets for these are quite expensive and are usually scarce. If you have no luck at the box office, agents such as Ticketmaster (☎ 0870 534 4444) or First Call/Keith Prowse (☎ 0870 906 3838) may be able to help—at a price. Never use touts.

Society of London Theatres tkts Ticket Booth
The tkts Ticket Booth on Leicester Square sells discount tickets for that day's performance. Beware look-alike 'half-price' ticket booths.

✉ **Clocktower Building, Leicester Square** 🕐 **Mon–Sat 12–6.30, Sun 12–3.30 for matinées only** ❓ **Cash (or theatre tokens) only. Service charge per ticket** 🚇 **Leicester Square, Piccadilly Circus**

Shakespeare's Globe
See the plays of Shakespeare and his contemporaries as they were meant to be seen—outdoors, with no amplification, in daylight (or 'artificial daylight') and in all weathers. In the standing area of the Yard food and drink may be consumed during the performances and the audience is free to banter (within reason) with the players, as they did in the original Globe back in Shakespeare's day. This is great fun but beware, the Yard is uncovered and no umbrellas are allowed. (► 69).

✉ **New Globe Walk, Bankside**

☎ **(020) 7401 9919** 🕐 **Season late May to late Sep** 🚇 **Mansion House, Cannon Street, London Bridge**

The Royal Shakespeare Company/The Barbican
The London home of the RSC is the Barbican Theatre, acclaimed for the design of its main theatre though not easy to find among the maze-like concrete ghetto that comprises the larger Barbican complex. A smaller theatre, the Pit, is also used for plays by many others as well as the Bard.

✉ **Silk Street** ☎ **(020) 7638 8891 for box office** 🕐 **Oct–May** 🚇 **Barbican, Moorgate**

(Royal) National Theatre
The 'National' are resident at the South Bank Centre and are much admired for the outstanding quality of the serious work they produce in one of three theatres; the Olivier, the Lyttelton or the Cottesloe. All have productions in repertory.

✉ **South Bank** ☎ **Box office (020) 7452 3000; information and backstage tours (020) 7452 3400** 🚇 **Waterloo** ❓ **A few discounted tickets for 'sell-out' productions are on sale on the day of performance from 10am onwards. Get there early as they sell out quickly**

Regent's Park Open-Air Theatre
This beautiful space has long been London's favourite alfresco venue, staging plays (mostly by Shakespeare) and musicals.

✉ **Inner Circle, Regent's Park** ☎ **0870 060 1811** 🕐 **Jun–Sep** 🚇 **Baker Street**

Dance & Music

Dance

Royal Ballet
(► Royal Opera House, below)

Sadler's Wells Theatre
Rebuilt in 1997, this is the premier London venue for touring ballet, dance and opera, attracting international companies.
🖂 Rosebery Avenue
☎ 0870 737 7737
🚇 Angel

South Bank Centre
Top-class contemporary dance groups perform here.
🖂 South Bank ☎ (020) 7960 4242 🚇 Waterloo

Classical Music

Barbican
The London Symphony Orchestra (LSO) and English Chamber Orchestra are both resident at the Barbican.
🖂 Silk Street, EC2 ☎ (020) 7638 8891 🚇 Barbican

South Bank Centre
A prime venue for orchestral and chamber music and recitals.
🖂 South Bank Centre
☎ Queen Elizabeth Hall/Royal Festival Hall/Purcell Room (020) 7960 4242 🚇 Waterloo

St. John's
This deconsecrated baroque church makes a superb setting for concerts, mostly of chamber music. There are excellent-value Thursday lunchtime concerts.
🖂 Smith Square ☎ (020) 7222 1061 🚇 Westminster

Wigmore Hall
London's favourite small venue boasts near-perfect acoustics and attracts very high-quality chamber music and recitals. Its mid-morning Sunday concerts are particularly popular.
🖂 36 Wigmore Street
☎ (020) 7935 2141
🚇 Bond Street

Opera

London Coliseum
Home of the English National Opera—who perform only in English. The English National Ballet perform here at Christmas.
🖂 St. Martin's Lane
☎ (020) 7632 8300 🚇 Charing Cross, Leicester Square

Royal Opera House
After over a year of 'darkness' due to redevelopment and expansion, December 1999 saw the new ROH building welcome home the Royal Ballet and the Royal Opera companies. It has now recovered from management problems to reclaim its former status as one of Europe's greatest stages.
🖂 Covent Garden
☎ (020) 7304 4000
🚇 Covent Garden
❓ Ring in advance for backstage tours

Jazz

Bull's Head, Barnes
The pub by the Thames is recorded as early as 1684. Since 1959 it has gained a world-wide repuation for modern jazz attracting musicians from all over the world. Jazz every night and on Sunday lunchtimes.
🖂 373 Lansdale Road
☎ (020) 8876 5241
🚇 Barnes Bridge

Church Concerts
One of the most enjoyable ways to spend your lunchtime in London is to join the capital's office workers at a church concert. These are prevalent in the City of London but of particular note are the concerts at St. Martin-in-the-Fields (► 75) and St. James, Piccadilly (► 67). Lunchtime concerts are nearly always free, but do try to give a donation.

Music Festivals

London boasts a lively calendar of musical events. On the classical side the most famous is the Proms (➤ 116), but others worth attending include the Covent Garden Festival (late May to early June), the Greenwich Festival (June) and the City of London Festival (June to July), which also includes jazz performers. See also Kenwood House (➤ 50).

The London International Jazz Festival lasts ten days in mid-November.

Jazz Café

This highly popular slick modern venue is home to many international jazz performers in the capital and also plays the contemporary sounds of Latin, funk, soul, hip-hop and blues.

✉ **5 Parkway** ☎ **0870 150 0044** 🚇 **Camden Town**

Jazz 'n' Pizza

London boasts two very high-quality jazz and pizza restaurants; the intimate Pizza Express Jazz Club and the spacious, more classy Pizza on the Park.

✉ **Pizza Express, 10 Dean Street** ☎ **(020) 7439 8722** 🚇 **Tottenham Court Road;** ✉ **Pizza on the Park, 11 Knightsbridge** ☎ **(020) 7235 5273** 🚇 **Hyde Park Corner**

Ronnie Scott's

Small and smoky, this is *the* place to see the best jazz in the capital. There are generally two sets per night, one at 10pm and the other after midnight.

✉ **47 Frith Street** ☎ **(020) 7439 0747. Booking is advised** 🚇 **Leicester Square**

Rock and Other Contemporary Music

Always at the cutting edge of many styles of pop and rock, London is a great place to see live music, from pokey, smoky pubs to the mega-venues such as Earl's Court and the Carling Apollo, Hammersmith Three of the best medium-sized places to see a band you've heard of are the Astoria, the Brixton Academy and the recently opened Ocean. Get a copy of *Time Out* to see who's in town. A good time is usually guaranteed at the following venues:

Borderline

Lively basement with an eclectic musical booking policy, where you can catch up on a whole host of new sounds.

✉ **Orange Yard, off Manette Street** ☎ **(020) 7534 6970** 🚇 **Tottenham Court Road**

Dover Street

London's biggest live music restaurant, seating some 400 people, where the musical menu is jazz, blues, soul and R'n'B.

✉ **8–10 Dover Street** ☎ **(020) 7629 9813** 🚇 **Green Park, Piccadilly Circus**

Half Moon, Putney

This is a famed music pub, just outside the centre but a great place to see up-and-coming rock and blues bands.

✉ **93 Lower Richmond Road SW15** ☎ **(020) 8780 9383** 🚇 **Putney Bridge**

Hope & Anchor

Popular tiny pub featuring bands just burgeoning on the scene.

✉ **207 Upper Street** ☎ **(020) 7354 1312** 🚇 **Highbury & Islington** 🚉 **Highbury & Islington**

Roadhouse

Heaving 1950s US-themed live-music bar with a mainly thirtysomething crowd getting down to blues, funk and classic rock.

✉ **Jubilee Hall, 35, The Piazza, Covent Garden** ☎ **(020) 7240 6001** 🚇 **Covent Garden**

Nightclubs, Cinema & Sport

Nightclubs

The London club scene is legendary, with many clubs changing themes throughout the week. See *Time Out* or *What's On in London* for details.

Tried and tested venues for older clubbers include Samantha's. The most reliable of the new wave is the Ministry of Sound. Less intimidating to the casual clubber, though still very style conscious, are the Café de Paris and Koko (formerly known as Camden Palace). Other long-established venues are Madame JoJo's and Fridge.

Cinema

For mainstream blockbusters and premieres go to the Empire and the Odeon (avoid the adjacent cramped Odeon Mezzanine), both on Leicester Square; the ABC and the Curzon Soho, both on Shaftesbury Avenue; or the Odeon Marble Arch with the city's biggest (conventional) screen. At the opposite end of the cinematic spectrum is the acclaimed National Film Theatre (NFT), at the South Bank. Look in *Time Out* for dozens of other interesting options.

✉ **National Film Theatre, South Bank** ☎ (020) 7928 3532 🚇 **Waterloo**

IMAX

For a truly spectacular wrap-around cinematic experience the classier BFI London IMAX Cinema on the South Bank, or the IMAX cinema in the Science Museum, located in the hi-tech Wellcome Wing (► 23).

Top Sporting Venues

Football

Arsenal Football Club

Very successful club, English Champions in 2004.

✉ **Highbury Stadium, Avenell Road** ☎ (020) 7704 4000 🚇 **Arsenal** ❓ **Due to move to new Emirates Stadium in 2006**

Chelsea Football Club

The team to beat in the new millennium. English champions 2005.

✉ **Stamford Bridge, Fulham Road** ☎ 0870 300 2322 🚇 **Fulham Broadway**

Tottenham Hotspur Football Club

London's most glamorous under-achievers.

✉ **White Hart Lane Stadium** ☎ 0870 420 5000 🚇 **Seven Sisters** 🚇 **White Hart Lane**

Cricket

Lord's

Home of Middlesex County Cricket Club, the MCC and venue for test matches.

✉ **St. John's Wood** ☎ (020) 7432 1000 🚇 **St. John's Wood**

The Oval

Home of Surrey County Cricket Club and venue for test matches.

✉ **Kennington Oval** ☎ (020) 7582 6660 🚇 **Oval**

Rugby Union

Twickenham

Home to the Rugby Football Union and, while Wembley is re-built, League as well as Union internationals.

✉ **Twickenham** ☎ (020) 8892 8877 🚇 **Twickenham**

Participatory Sports

At Hyde Park you can play tennis (near Lancaster Gate tube), go horse riding (☎ (020) 7723 2813) or just jog. There are also tennis courts in Regent's Park. Swimmers should head for Porchester Spa at 225 Queensway, which includes Turkish baths; or the Oasis, Endell Street, Covent Garden. Should a heatwave hit town, it's worth noting that the latter has an outdoor pool, as does Hampstead Heath.

Spectator Sports

In summer (June to late August) you can watch the quintessentially English game of cricket at Lord's or The Oval. In winter, football (soccer) is the national obsession, though for London's best (premier league) matches tickets are hard to get and very expensive. Another winter option is rugby union. See *Time Out* for details of all sporting events.

What's On When

Cockney Tradition

On the first Sunday in October, St. Martin-in-the-Fields Church is packed for the Costermongers Harvest Festival Service. Costermongers were old London market traders who elected 'Pearly Kings and Queens' as representatives to safeguard their rights. These quintessential Cockney characters (a Cockney is a true indigenous Londoner) are a marvellous sight dressed in their traditional extravagant pearl-button suits.

January/February

Lord Mayor's Parade (1 January): This procession of floats, bands and classic cars (from Westminster Bridge to Berkeley Square) attracts around a million onlookers.

Chinese New Year (late January–early February): Human dragons and firecrackers light up Soho's Chinatown.

March/April

(University) Boat Race (late March–early April): Oxford against Cambridge over 6km (3.5 miles) of the Thames from Putney to Mortlake.

Battersea Easter Show (Easter Sunday and Monday): central London's best funfair with an Easter Parade on the Sunday afternoon.

London Marathon (third week in April): some 30,000 runners, from world-class athletes to fancy-dressed 'fun-runners', pound the streets from Blackheath (Greenwich) to the Mall.

May

May Fayre and Puppet Festival (Sunday nearest 9 May): an annual celebration of England's first recorded Punch and Judy Show, staged in Covent Garden in 1662.

Chelsea Flower Show (late May): the world's best horticultural show, held in the grounds of the Royal Hospital.

June/July

Trooping the Colour (second Saturday in June): an inspection and parade of the guards honours the Sovereign's official birthday (apply for tickets well in advance).

Wimbledon Tennis Championship (last week June, first week July): you can queue for early rounds but it's advance ticket-holders for the latter stages.

Henry Wood Promenade Concerts (mid-July to mid-September): Britain's best-loved concert series occupies the Royal Albert Hall for three months.

August

Notting Hill Carnival (August bank holiday weekend): Rio comes to London with the biggest street festival in Europe.

September

Festival of Street Theatre (second and third week): a great time to be in Covent Garden.

Thames Festival: a celebration on the South Bank of the river, culminating with spectacular fireworks.

October–December

State Opening of Parliament (late October to early November): Pomp and ceremony as the Queen arrives at Parliament in the Gold Coach.

London-to-Brighton Veteran Car Run (first Sunday in November): a great spectacle as Hyde Park is crammed with Chitty Chitty Bang Bang lookalikes.

Lord Mayor's Show (second Saturday in November): London's best traditional street parade, from Mansion House to the Royal Courts of Justice.

Christmas Lights (mid-November to early January): Regent Street and Oxford Street glow with the latest festive creations.

Practical Matters

Before You Go   118
When You Are There   119–123
Language   124

Above: *Revellers in Trafalgar Square*
Right: *A Horse Guard*

TIME DIFFERENCES

GMT
12 noon

London
12 noon

Germany
→ 1pm

USA (NY)
← 7am

Netherlands
→ 1pm

Spain
→ 1pm

BEFORE YOU GO

WHAT YOU NEED

	UK	Germany	USA	Netherlands	Spain
● Required ○ Suggested ▲ Not required					
Passport/National Identity Card	▲	●	●	●	●
Visa (regulations can change—check before you travel)	▲	▲	▲	▲	▲
Onward or Return Ticket	▲	○	○	○	○
Health Inoculations (tetanus and polio)	▲	▲	▲	▲	▲
Health Documentation (➤ 123, Health)	▲	●	●	●	●
Travel Insurance	○	○	○	○	○
Driving Licence (national)	●	●	●	●	●
Car Insurance Certificate	▲	●	●	●	●
Car registration document	▲	●	●	●	●

Some countries require a passport to remain valid for a minimum period (usually at least six months) beyond the date of entry—contact their consulate or embassy or your travel agent for details.

WHEN TO GO

London

▬▬▬ High season

▭▭▭ Low season

6°C	7°C	10°C	13°C	17°C	20°C	22°C	22°C	19°C	14°C	10°C	7°C
JAN	FEB	MAR	APR	MAY	JUN	JUL	AUG	SEP	OCT	NOV	DEC

 Very wet   Wet   Cloud   Sun   Sun/Showers

TOURIST OFFICES

In the USA
Suite 701
551 Fifth Avenue
New York
NY 10176
☎ 1-800 462 2748
www.visitbritain.com

Suite 1510
625 N Michigan
Avenue
Chicago
IL 60611
☎ 800 462 2748
fax: 312 787 0464

Suite 570
10880 Wilshire
Boulevard
Los Angeles
CA 90024
☎ 310/470 2782
fax 310/470 8549

In Canada
Suite 120
5915 Airport Road
Mississanga
Ontario
L4V 1T1
☎ 905 405 1720

POLICE 999

FIRE 999

AMBULANCE 999

WHEN YOU ARE THERE

ARRIVING

There are direct flights to London from all over the world. London has two main airports, Heathrow and Gatwick, with smaller airports at Luton, Stansted and London City (Docklands). There are train links to Paris and Brussels, and good road links to the Channel ports.

London Heathrow Airport	Journey Times
Kilometres to city centre	15 minutes
	40 minutes
25 kilometres (15.5 miles)	40 minutes

London Gatwick Airport	Journey Times
Kilometres to city centre	30 minutes
	70–90 minutes
48 kilometres (30 miles)	60–75 minutes

MONEY

Britain's currency is the pound sterling (£), issued in notes of £5, £10, £20 and £50. There are 100 pennies or pence (p) to each pound and coins come in denominations of 1p, 2p, 5p, 10p, 20p, 50p, £1 and £2. Travellers' cheques may be accepted by some hotels, shops and restaurants. Travellers' cheques in pounds are the most convenient. Bureaux de change are common in central London, but they often offer poorer rates of exchange. Credit and debit cards are widely accepted.

TIME

 London is on Greenwich Mean Time (GMT) in winter, but from late March until late October British Summer Time (BST, ie GMT+1) operates.

CUSTOMS

 YES
From another EU country for personal use (guidelines)
800 cigarettes, 200 cigars, 1 kilogram of tobacco
10 litres of spirits (over 22%)
20 litres of aperitifs
90 litres of wine, of which 60 litres can be sparkling wine
110 litres of beer

From a non-EU country for your personal use, the allowances are:
200 cigarettes OR
50 cigars OR 250 grams of tobacco
1 litre of spirits (over 22%)
2 litres of intermediary products (eg sherry) and sparkling wine
2 litres of still wine
50 grams of perfume
0.25 litres of eau de toilette
The value limit for goods is 175 euros

Travellers under 17 years are not entitled to the tobacco and alcohol allowances.

 NO
Unlicensed drugs, firearms, ammunition, offensive weapons, obscene material, unlicensed animals, counterfeit and copied goods, meat and poultry.

EMBASSIES AND CONSULATES

Germany
(0870) 005 6718

USA
(020) 7499 9000

Netherlands
(0870) 005 6961

Spain
(020) 7235 5555

WHEN YOU ARE THERE

TOURIST OFFICES

London Tourist Board Tourist Offices:

Main office
- Britain and London Visitor Centre, 1 Regent Street
  ☎ 0870 156 6366

Other offices
- City of London St. Paul's Churchyard
  ☎ (020) 7332 1456

- Richmond Old Town Hall, Whittaker Avenue
  ☎ (020) 8940 9125

- Twickenham The Atrium, Civic Centre, York Street
  ☎ (020) 8891 7272

Useful websites:
www.visitlondon.com
www.visitbritain.com

NATIONAL HOLIDAYS

J	F	M	A	M	J	J	A	S	O	N	D
2	(1)	1(3)	(1)	1	1		1		1		2

1 Jan	New Year's Day
Mar/Apr	Good Friday, Easter Monday
First Mon May	May Day Bank Holiday
Last Mon May	Spring Bank Holiday
Last Mon in August	August Bank Holiday
25 Dec	Christmas Day
26 Dec	Boxing Day

Almost all attractions close on Christmas Day. On other holidays some attractions open, often with reduced hours. There are no general rules regarding the opening times of restaurants and shops, so check before making a special journey.

OPENING HOURS

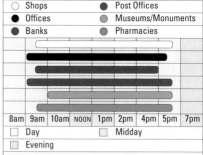

	○ Shops		● Post Offices
	● Offices		◐ Museums/Monuments
	● Banks		◐ Pharmacies

| 8am | 9am | 10am | NOON | 1pm | 2pm | 4pm | 5pm | 7pm |

| ☐ Day | ☐ Midday |
| ☐ Evening | |

The times shown above are traditional opening hours. Many shops in the West End open for longer hours and also on Sunday. High Street banks are open Saturday morning and bureaux de change are open daily until late. Smaller museums may close one day a week. When pharmacies are closed a sign in the window gives details of the nearest one that is on 24-hour duty.

DRIVE ON THE LEFT

TOILETS CHARGE

PUBLIC TRANSPORT

 Internal flights link Northern Ireland, Scotland, Wales and the regions with many of London's airports. London City Airport is in Docklands, less than 10km (6 miles) from the City financial district.

 Trains London is at the centre of Britain's rail network, with lines going out from its principal stations—north from King's Cross, northwest from Euston, east from Liverpool Street, west from Paddington, southwest from Waterloo, south from Victoria and southeast from Charing Cross. A comprehensive suburban rail network complements the underground.

 Buses London's famous red double-decker buses cover the capital in a dense network of services. A red bus stop symbol on a white background indicates that the bus must stop here (unless it is full); at a white symbol on a red background you must hail the bus by putting out an arm. Pay on board.

 River transport on the Thames is not as well used as it might be but there are regular services from Westminster to the Tower of London, Greenwich and Docklands. Sightseeing boats are frequent, popular and offer some of London's most memorable views.

Underground The underground, or tube, is by far the quickest way to get around London. Underground maps (▶ 72) are on display at stations, on platforms and on the trains themselves, and lines are named and colour-coded for ease of reference. Tube trains run from around 5.30am to around midnight.

CAR RENTAL

The leading international car rental companies have offices at all London airports and you can book a car in advance. Local companies offer competitive rates and will deliver a car to the airport .

TAXIS

 London's famous licensed black cabs (which confusingly also come in various other colours) are very reliable with specially trained drivers. Hail them in the street when the yellow 'For Hire' sign on the roof is lit.

DRIVING

 Speed limit on motorways and dual carriageways: **70mph (112kph)**

 Speed limit on main roads: **50–60mph (80–100kph)**

 Speed limit on minor roads: **30–40mph (50–65kph)**

 Must be worn in front seats at all times and in rear seats where fitted.

 Random breath tests may be carried out, especially late at night. The limit is 35 micrograms of alcohol in 100ml of breath. Never drive under the influence of alcohol.

 Fuel is sold in litres and available as unleaded, lead replacement petrol (LRP) or or diesel. In central London, petrol stations are few and far between but there are many open 24 hours on the main roads leading away from the centre and in the suburbs.

If you break down driving your own car and are a member of an AA-affiliated motoring club, such as AAA, you can call the AA (☎ 0800 887 766 free phone). If your car is hired, follow the instructions given in the documentation; most rental firms provide a rescue service.

PERSONAL SAFETY

London is generally a safe city and policemen are often seen on the beat (walking the streets) in the central areas. They are usually friendly and very approachable.

To help prevent crime:

- Do not carry more cash than you need
- Beware of pickpockets in markets, on the underground, in tourist sights or crowded places
- Avoid walking alone in dark alleys at night

Police assistance:
☎ **999**
from any call box

TELEPHONES

The traditional red phone boxes are now rare; instead, kiosks come in a wide variety of different designs and colours, depending on which phone company is operating them.

Coin-operated telephones take 10p, 20p, 50p and £1 coins, but card-operated phones are often more convenient. Phonecards are available from many shops. Hotel phones are very expensive. To call the operator dial 100.

International Dialling Codes	
From London to:	
Germany:	00 49
USA:	00 1
Canada:	00 1
Netherlands:	00 31
Spain:	00 34

POST

Post offices are open Mon–Fri 9–5.30, Sat 9–12. The only exception is Trafalgar Square Post Office, 24–28 William IV Street, open Mon–Thu 8–8, Fri 8.30–8, Sat 9–8. Post restante mail may also be sent here.

ELECTRICITY

The power supply in Britain is 240 volts.

Sockets only accept three (square)-pin plugs, so an adaptor is needed for Continental and US appliances. A transformer is needed for appliances operating on 110-120 volts.

TIPS/GRATUITIES

Yes ✓ No ✗		
Restaurants (service not included)	✓	10%
Tour Guides	✓	£1–2
Hairdressers	✓	10%
Taxis	✓	10%
Chambermaids	✓	50p–£1 per day
Porters	✓	50p–£1 depending on number of bags

Light: London is not renowned for its bright sunshine and the tall buildings create a lot of shadow, so pack plenty of 200 ASA-speed film.
Where you can photograph: Most museums will not allow you to take pictures. Check first.
Where to buy film: Film and camera batteries are readily available from tourist shops. Rapid-developing services are also widely available.

HEALTH

Insurance
Citizens of EU and certain other countries receive free or reduced-cost emergency medical treatment in Britain with the relevant documentation (European Health Insurance Card), but private medical insurance is still advised, and is essential for all other visitors.

Dental Services
Emergency dental treatment may be available free of charge if you can find a National Health dentist willing to treat you. A list can be found in the yellow pages. Dental treatment should be covered by private medical insurance.

Weather
Although not renowned for its sunny weather, the sun can shine a lot in July and August, when many Londoners take to the parks to sunbathe. Some sights involve being outdoors for prolonged periods when you should 'cover up', apply sunscreen and drink plenty of water.

Drugs
Prescription and non-prescription drugs and medicines are available from chemists/pharmacies. Pharmacists can advise on medication for common ailments. Pharmacies operate a rota so there will always be one that is open 24 hours; notices in all pharmacy windows give details.

Safe Water
Tap water is safe to drink. Mineral water is widely available but is often expensive, particularly in restaurants.

DISCOUNTS

Students and Senior Citizens Senior Citizens and holders of an International Student Identity Card will be able to obtain some discounts on travel and entrance fees. There are a handful of good youth hostels in London (▶ 102).

The London Pass This is a pass to over 50 top attractions as well as an option for travel on buses, tubes and trains. The aim of the pass is to fast track and save money at selected major attractions. The pass is valid for either one, two, three or six days. It also offers discounts on restaurants and leisure activities. For further information www.londonpass.com

CLOTHING SIZES

UK	Rest of Europe	USA		
36	46	36		
38	48	38		
40	50	40		
42	52	42		Suits
44	54	44		
46	56	46		
7	41	8		
7.5	42	8.5		
8.5	43	9.5		Shoes
9.5	44	10.5		
10.5	45	11.5		
11	46	12		
14.5	37	14.5		
15	38	15		
15.5	39/40	15.5		Shirts
16	41	16		
16.5	42	16.5		
17	43	17		
8	34	6		
10	36	8		
12	38	10		
14	40	12		Dresses
16	42	14		
18	44	16		
4.5	38	6		
5	38	6.5		
5.5	39	7		
6	39	7.5		Shoes
6.5	40	8		
7	41	8.5		

WHEN DEPARTING

- Remember to contact the airport on the day before leaving to ensure the flight details are unchanged.
- If travelling by ferry you must check-in no later than the time specified on your ticket.

LANGUAGE

The language spoken by Londoners is as varied as the ethnic and cultural backgrounds from which they come. You will hear many different accents in the centre especially amongst bar and restaurant staff.

Of the 'London English' there is a range from 'BBC-English' (the kind spoken with perfect clarity which used to be favoured by the BBC) to the broad Cockney dialect of the East End. Made famous by the likes of Henry Higgins, or rather *'Enery 'Iggins* in *My Fair Lady*, Cockney cuts out the 'h' at the start of words, and the final 'g' from words which end -ing. Statements of fact are also often confirmed by the use of the term 'innit?' (isn't it?).

The most famous aspect of the Cockney language is rhyming slang, an insiders vocabulary which was developed among street traders for clandestine communication, for example telephone becomes 'dog and bone', and may be abbreviated just to 'dog'! Below are a few examples. You may hear the occasional word in a locals' pub or shouted out at street markets. In the latter case it may well be tongue-in-cheek, a touch of local colour put on specially for British tourists as much as foreign visitors.

Don't worry if you don't get it. Most Londoners will be equally baffled! If you want to delve more deeply, however, you'll find whole books and even mini-dictionaries devoted to the language of Cockney rhyming slang.

Common Cockney rhyming slang

apples and pears	stairs
barnet (fair)	hair
boat (race)	face
daisy roots	boots
dog and bone	telephone
(h)'alf inch	pinch, steal
'ampstead 'eef	teeth
have a butcher's (hook)	to have a look
jam jar	car
loaf (of bread)	head
mince pies	eyes
my old china (plate)	mate, friend
plates (of meat)	feet
porky (pie)	lie
rabbit (and pork)	talk, chatter– usually meaningless
rubadubdub	public house
tea leaf	thief
tit fer (tat)	hat
trouble (and strife)/Duchess (of Fife)	wife
two an' eight	state/mood
whistle (and flute)	suit

Other common colloquialisms to be heard in London

Awright mate?	How are you?
boozer	pub (or person who drinks heavily)
bobby, copper, the (old) Bill	policeman
bovver	trouble, fighting
chippy	fish and chip shop
a face	a well-known person
geezer	man, person
guv	boss
fag	cigarette
innit	isn't it (at end of sentence and not meant as a question)
leave it out!	stop it
scarper	to run away
the smoke	London
the sticks	the provinces (anywhere outside London)
straight up	honest
sussed out	found out
wotcher mate	another familiar term of greeting
would you adam and eve it?	Would you believe it?

INDEX

accommodation 100–103
afternoon tea 9, 61, 93
airports 119
Albert Bridge 36
Albert Memorial 49
American Museum 88
Apsley House 32
arcades 106
Ashmolean Museum 90

backstage tours 110
ballet and modern dance 113
banks 120
Bank of England Museum 32
Banqueting House 33
bars 61, 97
Bath 79, 88
Battersea Park 12
Bethnal Green Museum of Childhood 110
Big Ben 19
Bloomsbury 31
Bodleian Library 89
brass rubbings 110
British Airways London Eye 33
British Museum 16–17
Buckingham Palace 34
Burgh House 43
Burlington House 64
buses 9, 121

Cabaret Mechanical Theatre 18
Cabinet War Rooms and Churchill Museum 35
Cambridge 79, 88
Canary Wharf 40, 41
car rental 121
Cenotaph 77
central London 31–77
Changing of the Guard 34
Chapel Royal 66
Chelsea 31, 35–36
Chelsea Old Church 36
Chelsea Physic Garden 12, 36
children's attractions 110–111
church concerts 9, 13, 113
cinema 115
City of London 7, 31
Clarence House 66
classical music 113
climate 118, 123
Clink Prison Museum 37
Clock Museum 42
clothing sizes 123
Cockneys 116, 124
concessions 123
Courtauld Gallery 37
Covent Garden 31, 38, 110
Covent Garden Piazza 18
cream teas 99
Crown Jewels 24
Croydon 7
customs regulations 119
Cutty Sark 84

dental treatment 123
departure information 124
Design Museum 39
Diana, Princess of Wales 49, 62
Dickens, Charles 14, 39
Dickens House Museum 39
Docklands 31, 40–41
Docklands Light Railway (DLR) 41
Downing Street 77
Dr Johnson's House 42
drinking water 123
driving 118, 121
drugs and medicines 123

eating out 52, 60–61, 92–99, 111
electricity 122
Elizabeth II, Queen 14, 62
embassies and consulates 120
emergency telephone numbers 119, 122
entertainment 112–116
Eros statue 63
events and festivals 116
excursions from London 88–90

Fenton House 43
fictitious Londoners 14
Fitzwilliam Museum 88
Fleet Street 42
food and drink 60–61, 108
  see also eating out
Freud Museum 43

gentlemen's clubs 67
geography 7
Gipsy Moth IV 84
government 7, 19
Greenwich 79, 82–84
Greenwich Park 12, 84
Guildhall 42

Ham House 87
Hampstead 43
Hampstead Heath 12, 43, 50
Hampton Court Palace 13, 79, 85
Harrods 44
health 118, 123
Highgate 45
Highgate Cemetery 12, 45
history of London 10–11
HMS Belfast 44
Holmes, Sherlock 14
Horse Guards 77
hotair ballooning 53
hotels 100–103
Houses of Parliament 19
Hyde Park 13, 45

Imperial War Museum 46
Inns of Court 9, 47–48
insurance 123
internal flights 121

jazz venues 113–114
Jermyn Street 48
Jewel Tower 48
Keats' House 43
Kensington 31
Kensington Gardens 49
Kensington Palace 49
Kenwood House 50
Kew Gardens 13, 79, 86

language 124
Legoland 90, 111
Leighton House 50
Lincoln's Inn 47, 48
Lloyds Building 51
local knowledge 52–53
London Aquarium 51
London Dungeon 54
London Planetarium (Auditorium) 54
London's Transport Museum 54
London Zoo 55

Madame Tussaud's 56
maps
  central London 28–29
  outer London 80–81
  underground (tube) 72–73
Marble Arch 45
Marble Hill House 87
markets 9, 108–109
measurements 122
Millennium Dome 82
money 119
Monument 56
Museum of Childhood, Bethnal Green 57
Museum of London 58
museum opening times 120
music festivals 114
music venues 113–114

National Army Museum 59
National Gallery 20
national holidays 120
National Maritime Museum 82
National Portrait Gallery 62
Natural History Museum 21
Nelson, Admiral Lord 22, 67, 75, 82, 83
Nelson's Column 31, 75
nightclubs 115

Old Royal Naval College and Chapel 84
opening hours 104, 120
opera 113
orientation 31
Orleans House Gallery 87
outer London 79–87
Oxford 79, 88, 89–90
Oxo Tower 63

Paddington Bear 14
Palace of Westminster 19, 48
parks and gardens 9, 12–13

Parliament Hill 43
passports and visas 118
personal safety 122
Peter Pan statue 14, 49
pharmacies 120
photography 123
Piccadilly 31
Piccadilly Circus 63
Pitt-Rivers Museum 90
Poets' Corner 26
police 122
population 7
postal services 120, 122
Postman's Park 13
public transport 121
pubs 9, 53, 61, 97

Queen Mary's Dolls' House 90
Queen's Gallery 34
Queen's House 83

Regent's Canal 13
Regent's Park 64
Richmond 79, 87
Richmond Park 12, 87
river trips 9, 111
Riverside Walk 31
Roman Baths 88
Royal Academy (of Arts) 64
Royal Armouries 24
Royal Botanic Gardens see
   Kew Gardens
Royal Ceremonial Dress
   Collection 49
Royal Hospital Chelsea 36
Royal Mews 34
Royal Observatory 83
Rugby Football 115

St. Bartholomew-the-Great 65
St. Bride 65
St. George's Chapel 90
St. James's Palace 66
St. James's Park 66
St. James's Piccadilly 67
St. James's Street 67

St. Katharine's Dock 41, 68
St. Martin-in-the-Fields 75, 116
St. Paul's Cathedral 22
St. Paul's Church (Actor's
   Church) 13, 18
St. Stephen Walbrook 68
Science Museum 23
senior citizens 123
Serpentine Gallery 45
Shakespeare, William 62, 70
Shakespeare's Globe and
   Exhibition 69, 112
Sheldonian Theatre 89
shopping 104–109, 111, 120
Sir John Soane's Museum 69
Soho 31, 70
Somerset House 37
Southwark 69
Southwark Cathedral 70
souvenirs and gifts 105
Speakers' Corner 45
Spencer House 70
sport and leisure 53, 112, 115
State Apartments, Kensington
   Palace 49
State Rooms, Buckingham
   Palace 34
statistical information 7
students 123

Tate Britain 71
Tate Modern 71
tax-free shopping 109
taxis 121
telephones 122
Temple Church 47
Thames Path 13
theatre 111, 112
Theatre Museum 71
time 118, 119
tipping 122
toilets 121
Tomb of the Unknown Warrior
   26
tourist offices 118, 120

Tower Bridge 74
Tower Bridge Exhibition 74
Tower of London 24
Trafalgar Square 31, 75
traffic congestion 7
trains 121
travelling to London 119
Trocadero 63, 111
Twickenham 79, 87

underground (tube) 121

Victoria & Albert Museum
   (V&A) 25
views of London 53, 97

walking tours 9
walks
   Chelsea 36
   Covent Garden 38
   Docklands 41
   Greenwich 84
   Inns of Court 47
   Oxford 89
Wallace Collection 76
Waterloo Bridge 9
Wellcome History of Medicine
   23
Wellington, Duke of 22, 32, 67
Wellington Museum see Apsley
   House
West End 31
Westminster 31
Westminster Abbey 26
Westminster Cathedral 76
Whitehall 31, 77
Windsor 90
Windsor Castle 79, 90, 111
Windsor Park 90
Winston Churchill's Britain at
   War 77
Wren, Sir Christopher 14, 22, 56,
   62, 65, 67, 68, 83, 84, 85, 89

YHA hostels 102
YMCA hostels 102

Acknowledgements
The Automobile Association wishes to thank the following photographers, libraries and associations for their assistance in the preparation of this book:

Banqueting House, London 33; **British Museum, London** 17c; **London Dungeon** 54; **Mary Evans Picture Library** 10b, 11; **MRI Bankers' Guide to Foreign Currency** 119; **Museum of London** 58; **National Army Museum** 59c; **Rex Features** 14b; **The Ritz, London** 60b; **Spectrum Colour Library** 24c, 43b; **V & A Museum, London** 25b

The remaining photographs are held in the Association's own library (AA WORLD TRAVEL LIBRARY) with contributions from the following photographers:

Stewart Bates 51cr; Theo Cohen 15b; Roger Day 8b, 23b; Steve Day 88; Stephen Gibson 13b, 74, 91t, 92/116; Richard Ireland 32; Paul Kenward 13c, 39, 42t, 44, 47b, 49t, 49b, 56c, 64b, 68t, 68b, 79, 80, 81, 84t, 89; Jenny McMillan 2, 18b, 64c, 117t, 117b; S & O Mathews 36b, 77r, 82; Robert Mort 6c, 8c, 9b, 52b, 53tl, 61c, 65b, 87, 122l; Clive Sawyer 40, Barrie Smith 5t, 6t, 7t, 7b, 8t, 9t, 10t, 12t, 13t, 14t, 15t, 16t, 17t, 18t, 19t, 20t, 21t, 22t, 23t, 24t, 25t, 26t, 46; Rick Strange 1, 9c, 20b, 35b, 40, 45, 51tl, 52c, 65t, 75, 90, 122t, 122r; James A Tims 21b, 26b, 37c, 50c, 69t, 69b, 86t; Martin Trelawney 5b, 67c, 85; Richard Turpin 57; Roy Victor 22b, 30, 31t, 31b, 35t, 36t, 37t, 38t, 41t, 43t, 47t, 50t, 51tr, 52t, 53tr, 55, 56t, 59tl, 60t, 61t, 61b, 62t, 64t, 72, 73; Wyn Voysey 6b, 19b, 34, 38b, 41b, 48, 63, 66, 77l, 83, 84b, 86b; Peter Wilson 27t, 27b, 67t, 70, 71, 91b; Tim Woodcock 42b, 76, 78; Gregory Wrona 12c, 16/17, 62b

Page layout: Design 23
Revision management: Pam Stagg

Dear Essential Traveller

Your comments, opinions and recommendations are very important to us. So please help us to improve our travel guides by taking a few minutes to complete this simple questionnaire.

You do not need a stamp (unless posted outside the UK). If you do not want to cut this page from your guide, then photocopy it or write your answers on a plain sheet of paper.

Send to: **The Editor, AA World Travel Guides, FREEPOST SCE 4598, Basingstoke RG21 4GY.**

Your recommendations...

We always encourage readers' recommendations for restaurants, nightlife or shopping – if your recommendation is used in the next edition of the guide, we will send you a *FREE* **AA** *Essential* **Guide** of your choice. Please state below the establishment name, location and your reasons for recommending it.

_____

_____

_____

_____

Please send me **AA** *Essential* _____

About this guide...

Which title did you buy?
  AA *Essential* _____
Where did you buy it? _____
When? m m / y y

Why did you choose an AA *Essential* Guide? _____

_____

_____

_____

_____

Did this guide meet your expectations?
  Exceeded ☐ Met all ☐ Met most ☐ Fell below ☐
  Please give your reasons _____

_____

_____

_____

continued on next page...

Were there any aspects of this guide that you particularly liked? _____

_____

_____

Is there anything we could have done better? _____

_____

_____

About you…

Name (*Mr/Mrs/Ms*) _____

    Address _____

_____

_____ Postcode _____

    Daytime tel nos _____

Please only give us your mobile phone number if you wish to hear from us
about other products and services from the AA and partners by text or mms.

Which age group are you in?
    Under 25 ☐ 25–34 ☐ 35–44 ☐ 45–54 ☐ 55–64 ☐ 65+ ☐

How many trips do you make a year?
  Less than one ☐ One ☐ Two ☐ Three or more ☐

Are you an AA member? Yes ☐ No ☐

About your trip…

When did you book? m m / y y   When did you travel? m m / y y
How long did you stay? _____
Was it for business or leisure? _____
Did you buy any other travel guides for your trip?
    If yes, which ones? _____

Thank you for taking the time to complete this questionnaire. Please send it to us as soon as
possible, and remember, you do not need a stamp (*unless posted outside the UK*).

Happy Holidays!

The information we hold about you will be used to provide the products and services requested
and for identification, account administration, analysis, and fraud/loss prevention purposes. More
details about how that information is used is in our privacy statement, which you'll find under the
heading "Personal Information" in our terms and conditions and on our website: www.theAA.com.
Copies are also available from us by post, by contacting the Data Protection Manager at AA,
Southwood East, Apollo Rise, Farnborough, Hampshire GU14 OJW.

We may want to contact you about other products and services provided by us, or our partners (by
mail, telephone) but please tick the box if you DO NOT wish to hear about such products and
services from us by mail or telephone. ☐